Healing Love

Healing Love

How God Works Within the Personality

Everett L. Shostrom
& Dan Montgomery

ABINGDON NASHVILLE

HEALING LOVE

Copyright © 1978 by Abingdon

All rights reserved.
No part of this book may be reproduced in any manner
whatsoever without written permission of the publisher
except brief quotations embodied in critical articles
or reviews. For information address Abingdon,
Nashville, Tennessee.

Library of Congress Cataloging in Publication Data

SHOSTROM, EVERETT L., 1921-
  Healing love.
  Bibliography: p.
  Includes index.
  1. Christian life—1960- 2. Love. 3. Christianity—Psychology. I.
  Montgomery, Dan, 1946- joint author. II. Title.
  BV4501.S452   248'.4   78-8294

ISBN 0-687-16739-6

MANUFACTURED BY THE PARTHENON PRESS AT
NASHVILLE, TENNESSEE, UNITED STATES OF AMERICA

In memory of my friend and teacher, Abraham Maslow.

—E.S.

To my parents, Charles and Anna Mae.

—D.M.

Acknowledgements

We express gratitude to Jane Leonard for her editorial contributions; to Shaleen Camery-Hoggatt for her diligence in typing the manuscript; and to Bobby Title for her assistance in preparing the index.

Introduction

Love heals. Fear destroys.

This book is about the power of love to heal the emotional wounds we have all suffered in life. Not that that's an easy thing to do, you understand. But we need the power of love in our lives in order to have peace, courage, and wholeness.

We believe that none of us is alone, no matter how desperate or dark our life seems to be. Deep in our core, the innermost part of our personality, is the power of love waiting to be discovered and utilized. Some would call this inner force an innate sense of freedom and dignity. Others would call it the presence of a loving God. We would say that it is both. For we believe that God loves us and that he desires to make us whole in body, mind, and spirit. Yet, it is the nature of his love to affirm our freedom and dignity. But the pathway to a life based on love may be blocked by many things.

We have all been hurt, betrayed, bruised, or ignored during the course of our life. And consciously or unconsciously our ability to trust the divine love in our depths may have been weakened. By learning to understand how our personality has been damaged and how our relationships with others have been hindered, we can again develop the courage to trust life and to love ourselves, others, and God.

9

This book is about ordinary people. The reader may well recognize himself or herself in page after page. While the names of the many people presented in case studies have been changed, the details of their lives are true. As authors, we share our own life experiences throughout the book. Our purpose is to make this a deeply human work that both elevates man and brings God down to earth. We wish to inspire the broken-hearted, impart courage to the hopeless, and give direction to those who feel lost in life.

Together we will walk through the valley of fear—those fears that disrupt our lives and paralyze our growth; but our journey will end on a resounding note of triumph and joy. We do not feel naïve or idealistic in our hope. Rather, we have both learned that people are deeply creative in bouncing back from the harsh blows that life can sometimes give. And the love of God is so tough and persistent that nothing can defeat those who learn to trust his guidance from the depths of their beings.

Ours is a vision of hope. The focus is on actualizing the Christlike potential within each of us. We offer not a new theology but a new concept of religious life, a concept that integrates psychological principles of growth with a biblical understanding of man's potential for greatness.

In a very real sense, we feel that he has inspired the writing of this book and that he will illumine your reading of it.

Contents

List of Illustrations

1. Encountering God

This book has been born out of the authors' shared vision of making the dynamics of human personality understandable to the Christian, or to anyone who is seeking to know more about life and personality.

Before we progress too far into the narrative text, we want to allow the reader to develop a sense of who we are as well as of what we are wanting to say. We want you to know us as persons and fellow-seekers in the adventure of life. In order to do this, we have each written a short vignette describing ways in which our lives have been touched by God. For each of us, the experience has proved to be life-changing and has led to, among other things, the writing of this book.

In the Presence of My Enemies—*Ev Shostrom*

Destined originally to be an Army of Occupation Troops, our 75th Division was instead committed to combat when the Germans made their last attempt to reverse the tide of World War II. I was a brand-spanking-new 2nd Lieutenant platoon leader. On December 13, 1944, my birthday, I went into combat with forty-eight men. When I was wounded seven weeks later, I had only eight men left.

Because of the desperately difficult conditions of combat in the middle of winter, that nearly two-month period was the most trying in my life. Again and again, my platoon was chosen to lead the wedge of the company in combat. Often we walked through six feet of snow. I was dead tired, and angry at the hunger, fatigue, and all the hardship of intense combat.

Then I was wounded by a German machine gun, and the rest of the company was pinned down. Cut off from my platoon, I lay in a field outside the town we were about to take—bleeding, afraid I would die. I asked God to save me, somehow. I promised that I would become a minister or do something spiritually significant with my life. Suddenly, there came a break in combat, and our company took the town. Soon German prisoners started coming from the newly taken town and saw me, hurt and badly bleeding.

There were many more German prisoners than remaining U.S. soldiers guarding them. The Germans swarmed by with their hands up behind their heads, led from far behind by one or two armed victors. Yet the prisoners voluntarily picked me up and dropped me off at a nearby German hospital. It had not yet even been taken over by U.S. Army medical troops. So, paradoxically, I found myself being nursed back to health by Germans. My "enemies" had cared for me even before my own had had a chance to do so.

This was the most dramatic moment of my life. My former enemies were now my friends! I had been taught by my training how awful these Nazi troops were, and now I found them to be compassionate human beings. This was crazy, I thought; I was taught that they were all devils! How surprised I was to find that every German soldier had emblazoned on his belt buckle "God with Us."

One of the kindest, most empathetic human beings I have ever met was a German male nurse, who by his compassionate caring demonstrated to me the power of genuine love, as opposed to military force. In a crazy war where values were turned upside down, I felt valued as a person by this nurse, a former enemy. Just a few days ago, we could have killed each other in combat! The polarity of friend and enemy had suddenly reversed itself.

This series of experiences changed my life. I had dedicated

myself to God and seen human beings in a new way. Before the war, I had been an accounting major at the University of Illinois. During my sixteen-month recuperation period in the military hospital, I decided that accounting was not what God intended for me to do.

I have sometimes wondered if perhaps I should have become a minister or missionary. And I have wondered for the last thirty years if psychology is the mission for which God intended me. I have always felt a deep camaraderie with the clergy. And I have believed that all of us, not just the clergy, can follow a mission outlined by God.

Dan Montgomery, a dear friend and Christian psychologist, is co-author of this book. He brings out the spiritual dimensions of my theory, grounding them with biblical references. He also shares his cataclysmic Christian experiences and insights on living an actualizing life.

Dan's freshness of approach to the Christian outlook and confidence in my ideas have helped me to have faith in the spiritual relevance of my work. Thus he has caused me to have the courage to examine whether I have at least in part fulfilled the promise I made to God over thirty years ago.

In this book, I want to share the essence of my work over those years—my theory and its psychological and spiritual relevance. In doing so, I hope to discover that I have been serving God's will.

The Rushing Wind—*Dan Montgomery*

I locked myself in a large room on the top floor of an old Methodist church. I didn't want to be disturbed on this warm, quiet summer's night.

My heart was expectant. I was seeking God.

For these past several months—ever since graduation from the university—I had been filled with a kind of awe and wonder. He exists—God exists! I had, only weeks before tonight's encounter, come to know him in a personal way. I had briefly walked with the Lord in my high-school years, but it hadn't lasted on my part. As a college senior I had made the

17

grand pronouncement: "God doesn't exist; we only make him up to counter our anxious feelings about an indifferent, impersonal universe." Now I was seeking to rediscover God.

"Oh Lord," I prayed as I sat expectantly in the dark room, "I'm so thankful for the tender way you have drawn me back in these last months. I want to walk close to you for the rest of my life. Please give me the grace and the power to do so."

Looking back on that quiet, reflective moment, I'm not sure just how I expected God to answer my prayer. But I certainly was not prepared for what happened next. The roar of a mighty, rushing wind filled the room!

I know that I would have been terribly frightened had it not been for the sensation I had of being bathed in love. The surge of warm, tingling feelings reached such a crescendo that I felt I could not contain the richness of such unrestrained love—I felt that such fire could consume me, or that my joyful response would reach the point of explosion. I suddenly cried out, "Stop!" And the sound and sensation immediately stopped.

I walked over to the windows, my old skepticism surging, to make sure that the wind I had just heard had not been from outside. It had not; the night was still. I became aware of the rapid throbbing of my own heart—I had been so startled by the rushing wind!

Now convinced that it was God who was in some strange way revealing himself to me, I returned to the center of the room, sat down, relaxed, and again began to pray. "Oh God, forgive me for being so scared. It is just that I never knew that you could manifest yourself in this way. I am ready now. Pour out your love. Fill me with your power."

Exactly as before, the room was filled with the sound of wind and my body was infused with a most profound sense of being loved. I felt as if wave after wave of joy were bursting across the shores of my being. How could such an inexhaustible ocean of power be so gentle, so tender, so caressing! Then suddenly: fear. I couldn't stand for another moment the ecstasy of such a love. I yelled, "Stop!" And all fell silent.

After several minutes, my breathing returned to normal. I

spoke to the Lord: "I do not fully understand the meaning of this experience. I am filled with awe. Your love goes beyond anything I could ever have imagined. I know that someday I will trust you so much that I will not feel afraid; I will not draw back when you express your love to me. Thank you for being so patient. I have much to learn. Good night."

With that I took a deep breath, found my way out of the darkened church, and drove home. "He loves me," I whispered. "He is so near—and he really loves me."

As a young person, I had turned away from Christianity. It seemed to be a religion of words only. There was much said on Sunday, but nothing seemed to come of it the rest of the week. I realize now that that was an oversimplification, but that is how it struck me then. And I had always thought of God as a very boring person who knew nothing of adventure and fun. I figured that if I really did encounter him, he would make me a boring person too! I had been an atheist, an existentialist, and I didn't need God.

Now all that was changing. I was experiencing God's love firsthand. Christ was now becoming the precious lodestone of my adult life.

Ev has called my orientation to religious life "cataclysmic." It is, in the sense that my encounter with God almost a decade ago shook my understanding of life to the foundations. It continues to have a profound impact on my life.

Yet, I am still aware of agnostic or atheistic problems with the existence of God. Many of the dilemmas that people struggle with make a great deal of sense to me.

But I have found over the years that I can doubt some things, question some things, rebel against some things, and still be a devoted Christian. Somehow the God that I know is not easily threatened or shaken up by my honest questions.

My growth as a Christian has at times been turbulent and agonizing. At other times it has been peaceful and quiet. I still cannot explain the mystery of growth. I chalk it up to two important ingredients: my own desire to grow, and God's ever-present grace and inspiration in my life. I have often responded to the Lord as Peter did: "Lord, to whom would I go? You have the words of life."

Ev and I decided to write this book as a shared statement of our Christian faith and as part of our ongoing exploration of a dynamic Christian understanding of personality.

We ask the reader to remain aware that, while we have much in common, we are still two distinct persons. We experience God in different ways. Ev has experienced him mostly through the living of an actualizing life. I have experienced him often in direct and perhaps mystical ways.

As psychologists, we are prone to quote Abraham Maslow, Rollo May, or Carl Rogers. As Christians we quote Theodore Runyon, Paul Tillich, Adrian van Kaam, Old Testament prophets, New Testament apostles, and Jesus himself. We hope the reader will find these combinations intriguing, as we certainly find them so. We have included not only our theoretical ideas but also experiential comments throughout the book, under the heading of "Author's Personal Comment."

So we invite you to come with us on an exciting journey into new realms of growth and self-understanding.

2. Your Growth Potential

Life is richest when we realize that we are all snowflakes. Each of us is absolutely beautiful and unique. And we are here for a very short time.

—Elisabeth Kübler-Ross

You might be asking, "Do I have to be a Christian to understand this book?" No, you don't. We simply believe that much of the psychological and social experience of modern man can be solidly grounded in a Christian understanding of the universe, so we invite everyone to explore the possibility with us. We believe many non-Christians can add meaning to their lives through an understanding of the themes developed in this book.

The Christian reader might well ask, "But if you're going to talk so much about psychology, won't that somehow undermine my faith?" If your faith is built on the foundation that learning to love God with your whole being, and learning to love others as you do yourself is the highest priority of the Christian life, then our message will affirm your faith. A psychological understanding of personality can contribute to the effectiveness with which Christians seek to live out their faith.

The purpose of this book is to develop a psychological understanding of personality that harmonizes with Christianity. We are also concerned with relationships between persons, and between a person and God. The question that emerges throughout the book is this: How can anyone, including the growing Christian, get the most out of life?

We have coined a term—"the actualizing Christian"—to describe an approach to living a Christian life based on awareness, honesty, and trust. We believe this life-style leads to the graced fulfillment of one's God-given potentials in life. It results in the full development of one's personality and the increased capacity to have intimate and enduring relationships with others and with God.

Actualizing is a lifelong process, not a final state or a rigid ideal of perfectionism. It is a vision of how we can grow throughout the stages of life. Bernadette Vetter speaks of the journey of actualizing as "an opening of new doors, a becoming, a probing, a going inwards to my center, a developing of relationships . . . every arrival a new beginning!" (*My Journey, My Prayer,* p. 18.)

We believe that the growth of many people, especially those raised in Western culture, has been limited by a lack of trust of their *whole* being—intellectual, emotional, physical, and spiritual.

For many people, "head knowledge" is the stuff of life. If it is not logical, rational, and objective, then it is not important. So these individuals have great difficulty experiencing their intuition or expressing their feelings.

For others, emotionality is overemphasized at the expense of clear thinking and responsible planning.

Yet others have difficulty when it comes to the body. They consider the body as somehow evil or at least neutral and fail to recognize the importance of the physical realm of human existence. One of the awesome affirmations of the Christian faith is that Jesus, the Son of God, expressed his deity through a human body. He clearly demonstrated that the physical realm *is* important and, beyond that, that it is to be valued positively.

Actualizing Christians rely upon important information derived from their entire natural and supernatural beings.

Using the Greek words from the New Testament, we could say that one learns to trust one's *soma,* or body; one's *psyche,* or rationality and emotionality; and one's *pneuma,* or spiritual sensitivity to God. All of these working together lead toward full and vital living.

The growing Christian learns to listen carefully to the messages of the body. A headache may mean we are too tense about life. A backache may mean we have chronically overextended ourselves. An ulcer may mean that we hate someone.

In actualizing, we learn to respect the wisdom of our own feelings and inner intuition. Psychologist Carl Rogers calls this the "wisdom of the organism." He writes:

> Time and again in my clients, I have seen simple people become significant and creative in their own spheres, as they have developed more trust of the processes going on within themselves, and have dared to feel their own feelings and express themselves in their own unique ways. *(On Becoming a Person)*

The actualizing Christian learns throughout life by continually exploring, expanding, and revising the meaning of his or her beliefs and values. In this open-ended approach, there is a desire to always grow beyond one's prejudices and premature conclusions about life. In psychological terms, one has an open perceptual field in which new configurations of meaning constantly emerge. In religious terms, one tends to be sensitive to the heart and mind of Christ—one is easily moved by the spirit of God.

Warming Up to Actualizing

Aristotle expressed a basic part of actualizing in his concept of *entelechy.* He viewed everything in the world as moving dynamically in the direction of completion, fulfillment, and actualization. Throughout the process, there is a vital link between the person's or thing's actual characteristics at a given moment and what will characterize it as a fully developed entity.

For instance, the acorn has within it the potential of becoming an oak tree. But it is only through the process of growth over time that the tiny acorn experiences transformation and actualization.

The idea behind entelechy is that the ultimate end or purpose toward which the acorn is developing is *embedded* in the acorn itself. The internal blueprint pushes, energizes, and guides the acorn in fulfilling its project of becoming a mature oak. In much the same way the person who is rooted in God is being transformed over time into the unique individual that he or she was created to be.

Although the actualizing process is pleasurable, it is not simply a hedonistic pursuit of fun or happiness. As Thomas Merton, a Trappist monk, once put it: "I feel like I am climbing the mountain of love on all fours, and I do not know where to look next!" There will be real travail for anyone who desires to become a genuinely actualizing person. But there will be real joy too—the joy of *being what one is and becoming more of what one can be.* This involves risk, faith, vulnerability, and adventure.

We need to learn to place a high priority on our growth toward authentic personhood. It will not happen automatically. We cannot change ourselves suddenly and drastically, even if we want to. Rather, real and enduring change is a gradual, steady process of becoming. It is nurtured by the courageous acceptance of our whole being—strengths and weaknesses, virtues and vices, talents and deficits. And, if we take it for granted, it may never occur.

Just as the athlete trains and warms up before beginning the hundred-yard dash, we must learn to warm ourselves up to the process of actualizing. It doesn't happen all at once. We need to discover our energies; heighten our awareness of the challenges for meaning that life is inviting us to embrace; and gain access to the inner, spiritual resources of the core of our being. Only then will we be able to live life with the sensitivity, wisdom, and vitality that is possible for us.

The Stable Core Within

Learning to live such a life requires concrete and specific guidelines. First of all, the spiritual core, the center of the personality, provides the function of lending stability to the always-evolving nature of the person. The physical appearance of the person changes throughout life in definite ways. The emotional responses change throughout a single day. The values and attitudes are altered over the course of weeks, months, and years. But the core self, the center of spiritual identity, remains the same. We describe this spiritual core of the person in the words of Roberto Assagioli:

> I recognize and affirm that I am a Center of pure self-consciousness and self-realization. This is the permanent factor in every varying flow of my personal life. It is this which gives me the sense of being, of permanence, of inner security. I am a center of awareness and of power. (*Psychosynthesis,* p. 119)

The spiritual core is an individual's God-given personhood, one's "God within." The Holy Spirit dwells here. The core reflects the fact that one is made in the image of God, and shares with God the capacity for awareness, choice, and intimacy. Whether that potential is fully realized during the course of a person's lifetime depends on his or her responsiveness to the wisdom of the core.

3. Compass Points
of the Self

As we move deeper into our understanding of human personality, we come to the fact that personality is dynamic, not static, in nature. Life itself is dynamic and changing.

Our central thesis is that human beings have four basic polarities: anger, love, strength, and weakness. These polarities come from the spiritual core of every person. They form a basis for understanding an individual's personality and relationships to others. These polarities can be viewed as the "latitude and longitude" of the self.

In Figure 1 you will notice that these feelings are placed at opposite ends of a line running through the center, or spiritual core, of the personality. Love is the polar opposite of anger. Strength is the polar opposite of weakness. What the reader must project into the figure is the dynamic quality of continuous movement. Even in the closest of relationships, love eventually gives way to anger. And for even the most confident or capable person, the sense of strength and adequacy eventually gives way to a sense of weakness or vulnerability. Likewise, anger that is expressed honestly and directly often generates feelings of love and tenderness. And weakness that is humbly experienced generates feelings of adequacy and strength.

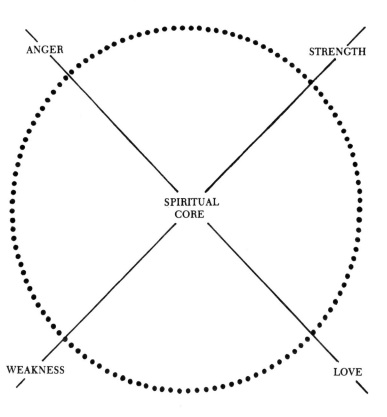

Figure 1: THE PRIMARY POLARITIES
The love/anger and strength/weakness polarities are the primary ones—the latitude and longitude of the self.

Love/Anger

The love/anger continuum enables us to be expressive all the way from *agape* love (the unconditional love that God has for

27

humankind) to strong anger (a rightful anger at the violation of human rights).

In his research on self-actualizing people, psychologist Abraham Maslow determined that they could express tender love or anger with ease. He also found that they were competent and strong, yet were keenly aware of their weaknesses. Thus, the actualizing life-style involves the dynamic and rhythmic experiencing of each and every one of these dimensions as they are deemed appropriate to every moment of life.

Both ends of the continuum must be experienced to live life to the fullest. To love someone is to be close to him, often giving pleasurable "strokes" or messages that he is regarded as precious. Love involves a warm, nonjudgmental empathy that reaches deep into the heart of the other. Parents often experience this feeling for their children. Or spouses for each other. Persons who have grown significantly in Christlikeness experience tender and consistent love for all of humanity—they reach out emotionally to men, women, and children wherever they encounter them.

But closeness also means "rubbing each other the wrong way" from time to time. And then it becomes appropriate to say "ouch" or "that irritates me." This is the function that anger serves in a relationship.

Ev has done research that indicates that many Christian married couples have a great deal of trouble expressing their anger to each other. They get angry, all right, but they tend to *re*press it rather than *ex*press it clearly. Anger that is repressed—or pushed out of one's awareness—usually comes out behaviorally as either depression or nagging. Therefore, couples that do not honestly level with themselves and with each other about their anger maintain only a pretense of a loving relationship. Underneath they remain irritable, frustrated, and most probably critical with each other in subtle ways.

Even the word "encounter" has connotations that portray both ends of the love/anger polarity. On the one hand, encounter can imply a warm and tender sharing between persons. On the other hand, it can mean a fight or skirmish, as in a hostile encounter between troops. The word captures two opposing, yet complementary, aspects of being human—the aspect of "being with" others in an empathetic way, and that of "being against" others in a confronting way. These two meanings are brought together when we speak of confrontation with caring. This is the kind of latitude that people need in order to develop honest, loving, and growth-oriented relationships.

In human relationships this dialectic is never fully resolved, for we are constantly alternating between being alone and being with others, between giving ourselves to others and rediscovering ourselves in opposition to them, between cooperation and conflict. The point is that *both* aspects are necessary for balanced, expressive human interaction.

One of the problems in many churches is the fear of open and direct communication. Many Christians have been taught to be polite and keep smiling. They do not know how to honestly and constructively express their disagreements, annoyances, or anger. Instead, they bottle it up inside. The perpetual smile, then, becomes a phony mask that covers up an angry heart. The irony is that the anger *does* come out, but in the form of gossip or dissension rather than creative conflict.

A pastor was recently consulting with Dan about a troublesome situation developing in his congregation. He revealed that some of the church members had been dissatisfied with his ministry over the past two years. He had heard through the grapevine that they were planning to split the church and set out on their own. When asked whether or not he had sought out the dissenting members in order to express his feelings to them, the pastor replied that he did not believe in sharing his feelings. "Pastors are not supposed to get mad or frustrated," he said. Dan challenged that assumption and suggested that if he leveled with the people, they might also level with him. If he shared his feelings of hurt, frustration, and anger with them, then they might share their feelings with him. Out of such honest expression of feelings could come new information and greater wisdom for guiding the church.

The pastor was reluctant, but chose to take the risk. Within the next week he and his wife visited the homes of those who had opposed his leadership. He shared his deepest feelings and concerns with them, then listened in turn to them. Much to everyone's surprise, the air began to be cleared of resentment and bitterness. The people involved began to breathe easier, owing to the relief of having gotten things off their chests. With a greater flow of information, everyone felt more confident in the possibility of a constructive outcome to the initial disagreements.

The pastor even stated that if the consensus of feelings came to be that he should resign from the church, he would do so in good conscience and with respect for the honest sentiment that had been shared. It looks as though that will not happen, because the members of the congregation have become much warmer and more open to one another as a result of the honest, ongoing exchange of views and feelings.

Strength/Weakness

In considering the strength/weakness continuum, we want to deal first with the two-edged sword of pride. We can easily be conditioned by our cultural emphasis on competition, industriousness, and performance to develop an exaggerated sense of self-sufficiency. Describing one side of the sword, Augustine believed that excessive pride was the greatest of all sins because it alone had the power to sever our humble reliance upon the Creator. So in one way, pride can cause a separation between our core self and God. Yet when managed artfully, it is healthy to have pride in one's strengths. That kind of pride is a wise acceptance and awareness of one's capabilities. Thereby, one can also gain an understanding of one's limitations or weaknesses.

No one remains "king of the mountain" indefinitely. Actualizing requires that each person, no matter how strong or gifted, accept that he or she is equally weak, often foolish, and makes many mistakes. The scriptures emphasize that "pride goeth before the fall" only to surface the reliable truth that actualizing one's strengths is possible only when one has the courage to become aware of one's weaknesses as well.

Author's personal comment—Dan:
Actually, dealing with pride has been very difficult for me. It is hard to share my weaknesses openly. This may be due to the fact that I have felt attacked by others over the years for some of the important values I have adopted. So I have countered by always building a case to show that I am right and they are wrong. I am tired of doing this. I am gradually learning that I do not always have to be right or perfect. Increasingly I am able to let down my defenses and share my secret fears, weaknesses, and needs.

A healthy and realistic acceptance of our weaknesses and limitations is the basis for humility. But in order to balance a genuine sense of humility in our lives, we need to cultivate an awareness of courage and personal power. This we would call the strength dimension of personality. To ask which polarity is the most important in living would be like asking which leg is more important in walking. They are both essential for living life fully—and each emerges rhythmically in daily living.

An interesting biblical description of such a life-style is found in Moses. We discover that he was *both* "the meekest man who ever lived" *and* a man of such courage that he led a nation from the Egyptian Exodus, through forty years of wandering in the wilderness, on into the land that God had originally promised them. Moses was so angry at the rebellious behavior at Sinai that he threw down and shattered the rock tablets upon which God had inscribed the Ten Commandments. The next moment, however, we find him interceding with God in a profoundly unselfish and loving way for the well-being of those with whom he had just been so angry.

So in Moses we meet a man who expressed the polarities of love/anger and strength/weakness to the fullest. We see a man who talked with God as friend to friend and yet expressed his feelings deeply and honestly to people. Even with God he expressed his feelings directly. At the site of the burning bush, he declared his fear, his lack of confidence, and his embarrassment at the prospect of becoming leader of the Israelite nation. So God promised that Aaron would speak for him to the people. Then when Pharaoh did not immediately release the Israelites as Moses thought he would, Moses angrily asked God what had gone wrong. Perhaps the scriptures pay such great honor to Moses partly because he was a person who gave all dimensions of himself so honestly to his lifelong encounters with God and people.

Author's personal comment—Ev:
A man who helped me understand much about humility and greatness was Abraham Maslow, who is often referred to as one of the fathers of humanistic psychology. Maslow dedicated his life to developing a psychology that paid tribute to human dignity. He did pioneering work that helped such important topics as love, joy, and personal fulfillment gain a respectable place in psychology and psychotherapy. It was with Maslow that I developed the Personal Orientation Inventory, the only published test for assessing self-actualizing tendencies in personality.

Maslow would often ask his students how many of them thought they would become great someday. When only a few would raise their hands, he would inform them that the greatest limitation in their lives was their lack of personal vision and confidence. He said that actualizing people believed in their strengths and greatness.

Actualizing Christians must experience their greatness as well as their limitations. This means feeling confident, strong, talented, and powerful, or weak, humble, and yielding as such feelings are appropriate to one's life.

Actualizing is cultivating a willingness to risk expression of the entire range of human feelings. "Contrary to popular belief," writes Arnold Lazarus, "the result of emotional freedom is not alienation or increased vulnerability, but decreased anxiety, close and meaningful relationships, self-respect, and social adaptivity" *(Behavior Therapy and Beyond)*. The actualizing Christian discovers and utilizes this principle.

The invitation that God extends to people is to become aware, feeling-full persons like himself. Both poles, and every level of intensity in between them, need to be developed so that we can come to experience life in the fullest and most sensitive way.

Instead of being one or the other, the actualizing Christian is balanced: both strong and weak, both assertive and caring. Growth involves increased refinement of the skills involved in interweaving all the strands onto the loom of one's inner calling from God. A striking and irreplaceable work of art emerges over time—one's unique identity which is in essence the gift of oneself to God's universe. All tapestry, being handwoven, is imperfect, as all human lives are imperfect. The imperfections do not detract from the original beauty, but rather contribute to the novel design of each person's individuality.

4. Journey Through Fear

Fear hath torment.
—I John 4:18

Recently in group therapy with Ev and Dan, a forty-year-old woman declared her frustration with life. "Next week I am going to a twenty-year reunion of my high-school class. Only I am terribly embarrassed because I have accomplished exactly nothing in the last twenty years!" She had raised several children. But she still felt lacking because in many ways her life had been completely dominated by her possessive and dictating husband. She had tried many tactics over the years, including fighting, pouting, or keeping silent. Now all feeling for her spouse was gone, and while the couple continued to occupy the same house, there was no emotional or intellectual communcation.

An important thing that the group fed back to her was the possibility that the next twenty years would not have to be a repeat of the last twenty. She could find the power in herself to change, even in basic ways, if she desired it enough to give up her fears and helplessness. This was hard for her to believe. The key turning point for her came when she finally admitted a deep desire to make something out of her life, and expressed a willingness to face her many fears. Among them were fears that she was too old to find an occupation, that her marriage would dissolve, that her children would reject her, and that no one could like her.

Fear and anxiety are built into human existence. We must all learn to cope with them. Psychoanalyst Karen Horney has emphasized the disabling power of fear by her term *basic anxiety,* which we define as free-floating fear.

> Through a variety of adverse influences, a child may not be permitted to grow according to his individual needs and possibilities. . . . As a result, the child does not develop a feeling of belonging, . . . but instead a profound insecurity and vague apprehensiveness, for which I use the term *basic anxiety.* It is his feeling of being isolated and helpless in a world conceived as potentially hostile. The cramping pressure of his basic anxiety prevents the child from relating himself to others with the spontaneity of his real feelings. (*Our Inner Conflicts,* p. 18)

Fear is the reason so many people get stuck in life and stop growing. Or, more specifically, inordinate amounts of fear cause a person to stop growing. Everyone experiences fear. It is how we handle the fear that is so important. Do we use the fear as a catalyst for growth, or do we become paralyzed by it?

We want to discuss the importance of understanding fear as being at the center of all the polarities in the deteriorating personality (as shown in Figure 2), and why this idea is so significant for this book in general. We have said that love and anger, strength and weakness represent four basic polarities. Man, however, is like the amoeba. The amoeba is a one-celled creature that constricts when a threat of danger arises. When fear is present in people, they, like the amoeba, often constrict to the center of the polarities. So it is with the deteriorating personality.

The resistance to expressing feelings is manifested by a feeling of fear. It is as if fear exists at the zero-point of the polarities of the core. This is the point of indifference, deadness, or apathy, where many people prefer to remain, thus avoiding risking feelings that are needed for being in touch with others.

People must often begin to express their feelings by

expressing their fear, for in the famous words of Franklin Delano Roosevelt, "the only thing we have to fear is fear itself." In expressing their fear of feelings, people paradoxically begin to risk moving out from dead center to the various levels of feeling expressions.

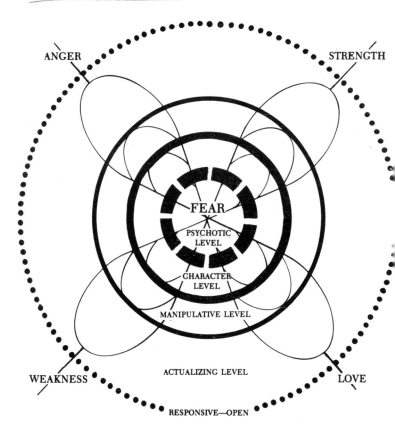

Figure 2: FEARFUL CONSTRICTION OF THE PERSONALITY

The Three Levels of Deterioration

When in the state of fear, we propose, one moves headlong into three progressively deteriorating levels. Figure 2 shows the actualizing level as the outermost ring, which one usually experiences as a child. But when one leaves the actualizing mode, moved by the fears instilled by parents, teachers, and society, one's life becomes more and more constricted.

First, as one moves inward from the outer sphere, one enters levels of less mobility, greater rigidity, and more severe "shut-upness." Second, as the pattern of fear becomes more and more severe, moving inwardly to each more tightly encased inner circle, the experiencing of the primary polarities of love/anger and strength/weakness becomes more and more constricted. And third, the center of the nonactualizing person is filled with *fear,* not love.

Further dimensions of Figure 2 to be understood are the circles themselves, which stand for the ego boundary of the person. The greater the fear the person experiences, the thicker the ego boundary becomes. For the actualizing person (the outermost circle) the ego boundary is open and permeable, thus enabling the person to be responsive to others and to the many elements of his or her life situation. Such a person can be emotionally moved by the feelings or experiences of others, and can also react to others with the full intensity of his or her feelings, without cover-up. If one gets angry, one can show it honestly and directly. If one feels loving, one expresses it clearly. Or if one chooses not to express a particular feeling, one is still fully aware of it. Vitality is not diminished, as it is with the person who is fearfully constricting awareness of all feelings.

The progressive levels in the process of deterioration we term manipulative style, character disorder, and psychosis. In each of these levels, the ego boundary becomes thicker and more rigid, as though the person were building a coat of armor or wall around the inner self.

Some of these terms may be new to the reader, but we suggest that they are viable ways of looking at human behavior that can enrich one's understanding of self and others.

Christianity is in accord with the claim of modern clinical psychology that not coming to terms with basic anxiety and fear blocks growth and breaks down relationships.

Manipulative styles, character disorders, and psychoses are maladaptive survival mechanisms based on fear.

The Downward Spiral

Dan directed a fifteen-week growth group in a church several years ago. In the course of several months, Stan, a fifty-year-old businessman, began to become aware of a lifelong pattern of fearing intimacy in relationships. His first marriage had failed because of his avoiding being close to his wife. But just as disturbing were his many relationships with others that he characterized as being polite but rather boring and meaningless.

In the group, Stan began to share his experiences as a child and teen-ager. He said that no one would ever take him seriously. He often longed for someone to talk to him about something of importance. But his family and friends would only tease him or ignore him. This served to increase his basic anxiety. He said: "If only someone had talked to me, I could have gained some self-respect and even learned how to talk back. But they didn't. I became real self-conscious, and I still don't know how to respond to people. So I avoid them whenever I can. I've shared more in this group than ever in my life."

Stan's body reflects his difficulty with relationships. It is tense and drawn. Poor posture and lack of bodily animation reveal the isolation and fear he experiences in life. Even his monotone voice declares the agony of years of feeling frightened, alone, and left out.

The way Stan learned to handle people was to keep his distance, withhold his feelings, blame others when things didn't go well, and withdraw into grim silence when he felt angry with anyone.

But with the awareness of his fear of intimacy, Stan made real progress in the group. He became increasingly able to feel emotionally close to others. He took more of an active part in building relationships. He even surprised himself by being genuinely tender and even charming as he became moved by some of the difficulties that other people faced.

Stan is like many Christians who spend their lives going to church, but who do not learn how to relate to people in a direct and caring way. But with awareness, courage, and practice, Stan has begun the challenge of opening himself up to new and exciting friendships. His group provided him with an atmosphere of caring that gave him the support to make the journey through his fears.

We could say that Stan's life-style was rigid enough to be called a character disorder, yet not severe enough to be a psychosis. If the early development of a withdrawn approach to life had run its full course, it could have resulted in complete emotional isolation from others. This would be clinically diagnosed as schizophrenia, the ultimate inversion on the polarity of weakness. So the anti-growth forces that interrupt human growth can range in intensity all the way from mild to severe. It is like that for all of us, for we are somewhere along the continuum from full aliveness and effectiveness in living, to emotional deadness and incapacity to cope with life.

The important thing is that we learn to be sensitive to our own growth as well as to the psychological and spiritual well-being of those around us. This means taking responsibility to make sure we are following the best pathway for a vital and meaningful life.

The actualizing person is relatively free to experience and express personal fears. Such a person is able to live from within along all the polar axes of his or her being. Few people remain in the actualizing process all the time. More common is the tendency to be actualizing part of the time and manipulative part of the time. However, if the person remains unaware of manipulative tendencies, they may grow like weeds and eventually overtake the garden of the personality.

Unfortunately, most people learn to relate at the *manipulative level*. This comes about when experiences that bring pain

39

and fear result in a tendency to live in a more controlled and calculating way. Since the open and direct experience of feelings makes one vulnerable in bearing one's heart to others, the manipulative person closes up and becomes less straight-forward in order to avoid any possibility of being hurt or frightened again. He or she relates to others primarily in mechanical and unfeeling ways, thus becoming less authentic, less spontaneous, and less creative than the actualizing person.

Manipulative behavior is stereotypic and compulsive, lacking novelty and choice. That is why it becomes a boring and tedious way to live and often leads to depression. As Ev has pointed out in his book *Man the Manipulator,* manipulation is a way of using others to get what you consciously or uncon-sciously want from them. But the person who exploits people as though they were things loses the capacity to enjoy intimacy and love in relationships.

In contrast to the actualizing person, the manipulator invests more energy in fortifying the ego boundary and less in living rhythmically and responsively. Even the body becomes tighter and less sensitive. It is as though in pursuit of security, the manipulative person retreats into a walled city and tries to hide there.

Next comes the *character level,* in which the person literally becomes a "character"—that is, someone who reacts in the same narrow, limited way to almost any input from outside. This level of functioning is even more emotionally constricting. The fear is greater than that of the manipulator, and the person is more thoroughly stuck in rigid behavior patterns. There is a real inability to learn from new situations or from life. Rather, the person reacts in the same stiff, repetitious way day after day, year after year. This is the level of most neurotic behavior. The games or manipulative patterns now reflect a rather grim, frozen stance against a hostile and threatening world. The walls of the self become still more thick and rigid. This level could be described as further withdrawal into a central fortress within the city walls.

Finally comes the *psychotic level*, the desperate "Custer's last stand" against a world that is experienced as overwhelming. Everything is subordinated to the task of psychological survival in this crisis mode of existence. Fear has completely filled the center of the personality. There is no room for love, hope, joy, wisdom, or peace. The muscles remain chronically tensed or flaccid, depending upon the specific form the psychosis takes. The behavior of the psychotic is bizarre and extreme. The person may hallucinate, repeat certain phrases incessantly, or sit in one position for days on end. Meaning and emotional connectedness to others have almost completely disappeared, so the psychotic must construct an entirely new reality based on fantasies or unconscious drives.

At the chronic psychotic level, life is restricted to the tiny dungeon deep in the recesses of the walled city. During the acute stage, or "psychotic break" with reality, the individual can no longer sustain the heavy investment of energy required to keep defenses going. Therefore, the walls begin to collapse and the self is lost in chaos, apathy, terror, or rage.

Much human suffering makes sense when viewed as distorted attempts to survive in a world that has been painful, frightening, and poisonous to the individual. Fear, the central mechanism that sustains the defensive stance, occupies the center of the personality.

In the deterioration process, the person makes the terrible journey downward from fulfillment to fragmentation, from purpose to chaos, from humanness to robot-likeness—from the image of God to the pale of nothingness. Manipulative behavior, character disorders, and psychoses represent progressively more involved systems whereby one tries desperately to win in a world that is perceived as a fearful battleground rather than a place for love and intimacy.

Søren Kierkegaard, the Danish philosopher, coined an apt phrase for this process, whether we are referring to the religious or psychological ramifications of it. He said that a person begins to suffer the misery of "shut-upness." Thus in shutting oneself off from the unfolding adventure of a

God-directed universe, one begins gradually to lose touch with the deepest meaning of one's life.

For anyone caught in the downward spiral of deterioration, the biblical principle "love casts out fear" is like a lighthouse in a stormy cove. It means that we are no longer lost. Life can get pretty tough, but we can find our way home.

5. Being Stuck

The mystics, in claiming that God is to be discovered in the self,
are well aware of what they are saying. It is by neglecting self that
so many people have become really incapable of finding God.
                                                    —Ignace Lepp

In the battle for survival, one of the ways of dealing with fear
is to rigidify one's response to life. Human beings have a deep,
instinctive need to be loved and affirmed. When they are not
loved, and are discounted instead—as inevitably occurs in
growing up—they experience great pain, hurt, and *fear*. In
order to survive, a person may adopt a specific defensive stance
in life rather than dare spontaneous expression and risk being
hurt again. One literally gets scared out of being oneself.

Such a person becomes like a piano player who gets stuck
playing one note on the assumption that this is the only note
that is safe to play. In this chapter, we will be discussing the four
primary ways that Christians get stuck playing one note, rather
than expressing the entire symphony of their personalities.

The fours types that evolve out of being stuck on the four
polarities are somewhat like characters one would read about in
a novel. They can even be seen from a humorous point of view,
characterized like comic strip figures. A psychological portrait
can have the fascination of a novel and the humor of a comic
strip. What we seek to do further is to explain the dynamics of
such behavior.

Each of us reflects some of this behavior and can grow from learning about it. We encourage the reader to keep a sense of humor as well as an attitude of understanding about such typical human foibles. We often grow most when we can laugh appropriately and with love at ourselves.

Sometimes there is a pain or fear in seeing certain things about ourselves. Our suggestion is that that kind of pain is okay—even essential if one is to grow. It is like coming out of a dark cave and feeling painful sensations in our eyes at the first rays of the sun. After awhile we become accustomed to the light, and the temporary pain is replaced with the permanent joy of seeing!

In organizing the presentation of the four primary ways that Christians get stuck in their growth, we wish to use the categories of the Striving Christian (strength polarity), the Helpless Christian (weakness polarity), the Critical Christian (anger polarity), and the Compliant Christian (love polarity). For each of these categories, we will develop the deterioration process from manipulative level to character style to psychosis. In describing these three levels, we will use commonsense words to explain the meanings of all clinical terminology.

The Striving Christian

Of the four primary distortions of Christian life, which also affect non-Christians, the pattern of the Striving Christian may well be the most subtle.

Doesn't everyone admire the Christian who is industrious, busy, and constantly on the go? Isn't it a great virtue to burn oneself out for the kingdom of God? Don't we praise the person who weathers every storm, overcomes every temptation, and always has the victory?

The striving Christian is stuck on the *strength* polarity. Somewhere along the line of personality development, this person received the message that work, personal achievement, and competitive performance are the things that make life meaningful. He or she is afraid of being judged as being inadequate or unworthy if perfectionistic standards are not

THE STRIVING CHRISTIAN

met. The corollary to this assumption is that play, fun, recreation, and the joy of intimate relationships with others are a waste of time. Hard, continuous work replaces love as the central goal of life. Achievement is the one note that the Striving Christian plays compulsively day after day.

Most probably, the Striving Christian was hurt early in life when he or she, like all children, felt psychological and spiritual hunger for unconditional affection and love from others. At an unconscious level, this person feels betrayed that this deep human need was not adequately met. Love was probably given only for being a "good girl" or a "good boy." This child was probably told not to be sentimental—that it is a dog-eat-dog world, so it is necessary to toughen up and get to work to have any success out there.

There is a saying that "God helps those who help themselves." Even though this saying has some wisdom in it, it can easily become only a rationalization for putting more emphasis on performing, accomplishing, and getting ahead, rather than on loving oneself and others. The saying appears nowhere in the Bible.

The Striving Christian suffers under the heavy burden of perfectionism. He or she is the Pharisee of modern-day life. Since the joy of being loved or loving others is lacking, one works oneself to death trying to appear worthy. It then becomes difficult for this individual to understand the grace of God. It becomes almost impossible to feel genuinely loved by God, because he or she is constantly giving attention to meriting or earning that love. But love is a gift, and, despite all the accomplishments, the Striving Christian has the worst time simply accepting it. So he or she jumps back on the treadmill of life seeking another project, thinking up another program, or contriving another emergency. Unconsciously, this person is still trying to please mom and dad and even God.

The striving business executive needs to have a perfectly efficient organizational machine in which persons are manipulated as though they were objects or statistics. The striving housewife compulsively cleans the house as though it were a museum showcase, not a home in which people enjoy living together. The perfectionistic student makes a ritual out of mastering technique, memorizing trivia, and making high grades. The striving church worker may become so preoccupied with "saving souls" that he or she neglects completely the deeper opportunity for understanding, loving, and growing in relationships with other people. Unfortunately, self-awareness and sensitivity to others are often lost in the struggle to achieve perfection. One remains a spiritual infant.

There is another important dimension to this stuckness. The Striving Christian has been given the idea that always acting strong is a virtue, and that experiencing one's weakness, limitation, or vulnerability is a humiliating experience. Indeed, he or she was probably embarrassed as a child or young person for disclosing personal fears, doubts, hurts, and faults. So instead of admitting and confessing needs and weaknesses to others, he or she has learned to bottle everything up inside. This person develops a psychological rigidity that other people can sense. Especially spouse, children, and colleagues will sense the tenseness, irritability, and distance. One avoids honest sharing with one's family and mainly invests energy in solitary projects.

The inner attitudes that a person lives by are inevitably reflected physically. The body of the Striving Christian is often stiff and rigid. Tension is stored in the neck and shoulder muscles, as well as around the area of the jaw. Rather than walking with a relaxed and natural gait, he or she develops a hurried, tense walk that reflects the inner need to always appear busy and productive. Psychosomatic symptoms such as high blood pressure, chronic muscular tension, migraine headache, or lower back pain often accompany this style of living. The Christian who adopts the striving life-style might blame the disorders of the body on the devil. He or she might rationalize this physical deterioration by thinking: "Look how much I am doing for God. The devil must be punishing me for being such a hard-working Christian." What one does not recognize is that the one who is punishing and abusing the body

47

that God fashioned is oneself. The Striving Christian is so caught up in seeking status, wealth, or acclaim that he or she constantly ignores the God-given warning signs of a body that is gradually breaking down long before the Lord intended it to.

But rather than own up to one's limitations and take responsibility to give and receive love without the heavy criterion of achievement and performance, the Striving Christian is off to another convention, off to buy another piece of property, off to preach another sermon, or off to start another program.

Author's personal comment—Ev:

I can identify with the Striving Christian. Several weeks ago I spent a weekend in a self-discovery group. Each person had a chance to express to the group the goal in life that had been most important. The symbol that I thought of was an eagle on top of a mountain peak. It seems that most of my life I have tried to get to the top of the mountain, but now I find that it is a very lonely place to be.

After we had shared our life goal with the group, we had a chance to role-play an opposite kind of experience. For me, it was becoming a little boy again and putting my head in the lap of a woman who role-played a kind and loving mother. I was moved to tears. I realized that I had not gotten that kind of love as a youngster, and that the attention I had received was mostly for doing things well and performing or earning my way.

So I have spent many of my adult years doing just that. I hope that with my new awareness I can relax more in life and take things more as they come instead of wearing myself out trying to make them happen. I am slowly learning how to love myself whether I achieve or not.

When the genuine strength of the actualizing Christian becomes distorted into a *manipulative pattern,* it is expressed as inflexible *striving and achieving.* This is what we have just described. When it deteriorates even further, to the *character level,* the person develops a *rigid personality.*

48

The rigid personality strives to appear strong, competent, and capable at all times, and becomes a workaholic. As if this were not enough, this person continually dictates to others how they too ought to work themselves to death, judging them for being less dedicated than he or she is. Therefore, such an individual becomes more and more isolated from friends and colleagues, and tramples on other people's feelings without the slightest awareness of what has been done. Having lost sensitivity to the gentle promptings of the Holy Spirit, the rigid person may set out to accomplish very worthy goals but in the process do much damage and destruction because of this steamroller approach to life.

Since this person is afraid to feel the fears, anxieties, and weaknesses that are part of everyone's existence, an almost frantic preoccupation with busyness eats up the time and energy that could go into prayer, meditation, and quiet recollection that would enable one to discern once again the still small voice of the Lord. The rigidly striving Christian has never learned that the grace of God enables one to share openly and honestly one's deepest fears, doubts, and inadequacies. Perhaps only through the ultimate outcome of this life-style—heart attack, ulcers, or nervous breakdown —will one finally admit and humbly accept one's limitations. Perhaps only then will one know that the love of God does not depend on any project one could ever accomplish. Perhaps then one can be delivered from the do-get-go syndrome, which, like a giant leech, has sucked the life energies out of many a well-intentioned Christian.

As the Striving Christian approaches the *psychotic* stage, the behavior becomes characterized as manic, or extremely *excitable*. One is obsessed with unrealistic feelings of elation and an exaggerated sense of power. A frenzied compulsion for constant activity develops, and all sense of rhythm and Spirit-led direction in life is lost. There is no time for rest, recreation, or renewal. There is only a blinding blur of busyness in the striving to maintain the illusion of strength that has dominated this life.

Our culture actually encourages the Striving Christian in this self-destructive pace. One may be given a plaque for the most sales, a raise in salary for getting so much work done, or a banquet at which selfless efforts for the corporation or church are extolled. But in the end, the striver will suffer an early death and a disrupted family life.

We must recognize how far such a life-style departs from the truly biblical principle of resting and trusting in the Lord for everything that concerns our day-to-day living. As the Psalmist says:

> Trust in the Lord, and do good;
> > so you will dwell in the land, and
> > > enjoy security. Take delight in the Lord,
> > and he will give you the desires of your heart.
>
> Commit your way to the Lord;
> > trust in him, and he will act. . . .
>
> Be still before the Lord, and wait
> > patiently for him.
> > > (Psalm 37:3-5, 7*a* RSV)

Should you find yourself described in this section, be aware that there are ways for getting out of the rut of the striving life-style. Probably the most effective ways are to experience genuine love through your prayer life with God, or through your relationships with others. There is no doubt that you will have to reevaluate your priorities in life. Yet this can pave the way for some exciting discoveries.

Another good direction is to begin sharing some of your weaknesses and fears with friends, spouse, or family. Of course, this means risking what other people might think of you. But it also means that you are fed up with giving them a false impression and that you are now ready to disclose more of your real feelings, values, and desires. As you become more "human"—that is, balanced in experiencing both strength and weakness, both confidence and vulnerability—chances are that people will see you as more down-to-earth and approachable.

Nothing ever turns out right!

ebody take care of me!

d, why don't you
ke everything O.K.?

Tell me what to do.

I'm sorry.

Protect me.

Poor me.

I can't.

Pray for me.

Help.

It's no use anyway.

THE HELPLESS CHRISTIAN

51

Then you can know that the relationships you develop with others are real and genuine. We invite you also to open your deepest self to God, since he knows everything about you and loves you perfectly! Learn to love him back, not for what you might get from him, but just because he is so precious and lovable.

The Helpless Christian

The Helpless Christian is in the same boat with the rest of humanity in having weaknesses. The only difference is that even when a trusting relationship with God has been established, the Helpless Christian still feels the fear of being overwhelmed by life. This person feels that he or she hardly has the right to exist, much less grow. The Helpless Christian is stuck on the *weakness* polarity. Out of a sense of fear, the Helpless Christian distorts a religious commitment by remaining infantile and dependent.

This person's fear takes one of two forms. First, one may see God as the Great Rescuer and so stay helpless and continually wait for God's help. Or, second, one may feel so overwhelmed by God because he is so big and by contrast one is so small that there is nothing else to do except sit shaking in one's boots in his presence. Either way, fear blocks growth. This person is unconsciously relating to God in the same manipulative ways that he or she has learned to relate to others.

The helpless person has never learned to stand on his or her own feet. The body structure often reflects this in that the upper torso is often somewhat caved in, making the person appear fragile and collapsed.

The Helpless Christian may experience a very nice payoff for infantile and dependent behavior. There are many people who would like nothing better than to constantly rescue and take care of such a needy person. So the individual secretly enjoys the big fuss that is made over his or her difficulties, needs, and problems. If one plays dumb and does not learn to think for oneself, then others can be tricked into doing all the thinking. If one never has enough faith for anything, then others can be made to do the praying. If one is not willing to face life and learn to cope with it, then others can be hooked into giving advice, making decisions, and taking all the responsibility that should rightfully be one's own. So the helpless Christian says, "I cannot do it; I give up." And the rescuers say, "That's all right; we will do it for you."

Since getting in touch with one's own strength and adequacy will mean accepting new responsibility, the Helpless Christian may prefer to continue seducing others into doing the thinking, feeling, and acting. Of course, one unknowingly pays the terrible price of remaining a psychological and spiritual infant throughout life.

The other factor that may exert an unconscious influence on the attitudes and behavior of the helpless person may be early traumatic experiences with family or peers. It is highly probable that the person has felt overwhelmed, humiliated, or severely taken advantage of while growing up. Therefore, he or she no longer trusts anyone. One does not even trust oneself, because there is a residual feeling of terror and helplessness about not being able to cope with life on one's own.

Karen is a college student in her early twenties. Her life had been one bad experience after another and had left her feeling incompetent, lazy, and destined to be a failure. In counseling she revealed that her father had made sexual overtures to her during the years of puberty. As a teen-ager, she finally confronted her dad with her feelings of resentment and hatred. At last that stopped his sexual advances. But Karen has carried with her into her adult Christian life the residual feelings of shame and embarrassment, as well as a pattern of sexual promiscuity with men. Having never experienced an emotionally reliable relationship with her father, she finds it extremely difficult to understand other men. She is therefore an all too easy mark for those who would sexually exploit her.

In deciding to face her life, she has experienced a new hope and discovered a deep desire to amount to something. She has begun to take an active interest in determining how things will turn out for her, and is surprised that her choices can make such a big difference. No longer willing to be bound by her former fear of men, she has accepted that she had a poor relationship with her dad but recognizes that he is not the only type of man in the world. She has begun to build friendships with men that are genuine and supportive and allow her the dignity of being herself. For the first time in her life, she is taking an interest in doing well in school and in disciplining her time and energies in order to reach long-term goals of vocational excellence.

Then one day recently, after many months of growth, Karen made the most exciting discovery of all. "I am really loved. God loves me. And I can tell that some of my friends love me. And I am starting to love myself!" she proclaimed. It is still not easy for her, but she is making real progress in climbing out of the rut of helplessness and apathy.

At the *manipulative level,* the helpless Christian uses tactics of *withdrawal* and *avoidance* in order to escape the demands of responsible growth and self-direction.

At the *character level,* where Karen had found herself to be, the individual becomes cold, aloof, and emotionally detached from others. In psychological terms, we would say that the person is developing a schizoid character. In lay terms, we could say that the person is becoming *lifeless* and devoid of feeling. Having at some point felt a denial of the right to a fulfilling life, he or she is now determined never to again feel the pain of betrayal. Thus one psychologically locks oneself into solitary confinement and becomes numb to life, avoiding relationships and taking comfort in a hermit-like life where there is no emotional energy invested in another living thing except maybe a dog or a cat.

The passion, the interest or excitement with life, and the vision for fulfillment of one's destiny are all gone. Encountering such an individual, one wonders if there is a person at all inside the stiff, fortified body.

At the *psychotic stage,* helpless people melt silently into schizophrenia or an ultimate kind of "shut-offness" from the world. Not having learned how to live in the real world, they create a world of their own.

54

Going further, they regress to an earlier, totally dependent form of infantile behavior, relying on forces outside themselves for even the most simple bodily needs. This is both an alarming and depressing picture. Yet it is happening in people's lives.

If you find some of these tendencies unfolding in your own life, we urge you to begin reversing the pattern, just as Karen and many others like her have. The material throughout this book, coupled with your own desire and prayer, ought to provide you with many good options for growing out of the rut of being a Helpless Christian.

If you feel that pressures in your own personality make it impossible to grow or change in healthy directions, then it would be wise for you to prayerfully seek a relationship with a competent professional counselor or therapist. Many people nowadays are benefiting from several weeks or months of individual or group counseling or therapy with a qualified professional.

The Critical Christian

Blaming and *attacking* are a more aggressive form of *manipulation* used in relationships by Critical Christians. Because of the many times such persons have been hurt, they fixate on being angry and punitive, believing that consistently blaming and attacking others will keep them from ever being hurt again. Being hurt is the Critical Christian's greatest fear. So, paradoxically, he or she becomes the aggressor in hurting others first to keep from being hurt. This perpetuates a vicious cycle.

While being in good contact with the polarities of anger and strength, the Critical Christian is out of touch with the complementary dimensions of love and weakness. In fact, he or she is stuck on the *anger* polarity and cannot allow into awareness feelings of tenderness or humility because they threaten the rigid pattern of always being in control and being right.

When anything happens that the Critical Christian does not like, he or she compulsively seeks to find fault with others, God,

THE CRITICAL CHRISTIAN

or the world. Critical Christians enjoy bullying others into believing that their way is the only way. A closely associated strategy is judging others—constantly pointing out what they should be or say or do and where they have gone wrong.

Because the Critical Christian is basically angry at the world, he or she usually communicates with others in a rather brusque way. However, the same dynamic of attacking and blaming may be carried on with a smile and an artificial appearance of being a nice guy. Sometimes the Critical Christian just complains and whines constantly about not liking this or that.

As a child, the critical person could well have received the kind of harsh, judgmental treatment he or she now dishes out to others. Much psychological research shows that children learn many of their basic styles of relating by modeling themselves on the way that their parents or other authority figures relate to them. For instance, there is a high probability that children who have been physically or psychologically abused by parents will in turn abuse their own children, unless specific therapeutic intervention gives them new alternatives that they never had a chance to learn.

Chances are the critical person experienced real fear, helplessness, and torment in childhood. This could have been inflicted by insecure parents, jealous brothers or sisters, exploitative relatives, or bullying peers. But at some point, the pain reached such a crescendo that the person reversed roles—becoming the persecutor rather than the victim—and spent the rest of his or her life taking out the frustration, hostility, and pain on others.

When people living out a punitive style of relating become Christians, there is a high probability that they will unconsciously contaminate their understanding of God and other people. The contamination is a result of the old hurts and the hostility that they generated within. The irony, then, is that Critical Christians rationalize such attitudes and behavior by believing that God is the one who is angry, harsh, and judgmental of everyone. This supposedly excuses them for their own hostile behavior. This type of individual might even believe that he or she is an emissary of God, sent to dispense God's wrath on others. One, therefore, feels quite smug in laying heavy demands upon others and becoming a hard taskmaster in telling others how to be holy and live up to God's supposed expectations.

A noticeable pattern for the Critical Christian is the preoccupation with ritual, rule, and regulation. In the zeal to serve God, he or she becomes guilty of destroying the spirit of love and gentleness that characterizes true Christian behavior with a dogmatic and almost vicious concern with the letter of the law.

Author's personal comment—Dan:

I can recognize parts of myself in the Critical Christian. For several years after my Christian conversion, I was intolerant and impatient with anyone who saw things differently from me. I felt that I had all the answers about God, life, and other people's behavior.

I am now aware of many people who felt hurt and misunderstood by my brash approach to life. They felt that I judged them harshly. I am gradually developing a more gentle life-style that enables me to relate genuinely to people who are quite different from me.

The Critical Christian in the depths of his or her being is a frightened child. In order to grow, one must discover the pain, confusion, and anxiety that one has tried to cover up with arbitrary rightness and blustering about. One will have to risk venturing out into relationships less armed and armored; to experience and accept the vulnerability of showing one's Achilles' heel and baring one's heartfelt tenderness to others; and to give up one's tense demandingness about how one thinks everyone should be and accept them more as they are. This person will have to forgive those who have harmed him or her in the past, and move on to live out the rest of life in a positive and fulfilling way.

If the Critical Christian does not experience a change of heart in order to grow out of his or her manipulative rut, then he or she will probably deteriorate further into the character and perhaps psychotic levels of that same rut.

At the *character level,* the manipulative tactics of blaming and attacking become frozen into a life-style based upon *punishing* self or others. In psychological terms, we would call such a condition either masochistic (self-punishing) or sadistic (punishing others). Sometimes these terms have been presented only in connection with sexual relationships, but that is not our intention here. Rather, the style of punishing self or others describes critical people's total orientation to life—they live to make themselves and others miserable in every conceivable way.

Because such people have not tasted the joy of open and intimate friendships, they unconsciously crave stimulation of some kind. And, usually by accident, they discover somewhere in their development that feelings of irritation, hostility, and misery provide enough stimulation to bring some meaning, however distorted, to their lives. We might say they become addicted to negative feelings in order to fill the vacuum of having seldom or never experienced the positive feelings of peace, love, and joy.

This is very similar to a situation in which a young child feels ignored or neglected and then, by accident, does something disruptive that results in a spanking. The child does not mind the spanking, though, because at least he or she now has captured the attention of those around. So it becomes easy and rewarding for the child to develop a life-style based on making others miserable: the child will at least continually receive the stimulation that comes from being the center of attention. In this case, the child is willing to accept the threats, shouting, or spanking. What makes it all worthwhile is the captive audience. At least he or she feels significant, if not loved.

The life-style described above is more sadistic in that the person unconsciously derives pleasure from other people's discomfort and misery. He or she becomes the kind of individual who delights in destroying other people's joy and can always find something about which to complain. This individual avoids close interpersonal relationships, and even sabotages them by general pessimism and fault-finding.

The masochistic style of punishing is more directed toward one's self. The person feels frustrated and angry about life, probably from having been abused or exploited by someone. But instead of expressing anger directly at the person or persons who did the exploiting, one tends to "beat oneself up." An example is Albert, a construction worker, who was ignored often during childhood. The main feedback he received from his parents was discounting and critical. Now as an adult, Albert tends to feel guilty and unworthy even though he conscientiously tries to live the Christian life. He feels that God is always finding fault with him.

Albert is not directly aware of his anger toward his parents and even toward God. Rather, he has the appearance of being very meek and gentle. But he feels spiteful and angry underneath it all and is constantly taking out his rage on himself.

Albert demands of himself that he perform exacting and painful rituals in order to please God and prove himself worthy of God's love. At times he will fast for days, or lie prostrate before an altar praying for hours. But none of this helps. It just provides the stimulation that he is used to experiencing in life: feeling miserable, wretched, and short-changed is all he has ever known. So he contaminates his present relationship with the Lord and others with his need to be a suffering martyr.

The masochistic Christian gladly bears the crosses of life—even invents extra crosses to carry—in order to unconsciously inflict self-punishment. It is the only life he or she knows.

At the *psychotic level,* the repressed *spitefulness* of the punitive person builds up painfully, takes an opposite turn, and explodes against the world. He or she has practiced for years the art of self-torture and frustration. Now the psychotic critical person finally unloads his or her reservoir of resentment, spite, and rage. The explosion will inevitably be destructive to self and others, maybe even to the extent of homicide. This is because the critical person has been stuck for so long on the anger polarity of feeling that he or she has not cultivated feelings of love and tenderness toward others. Without empathy, the person must express anger without any kind of sensitivity. He or she has never learned to experience and express the many different levels of anger in an actualizing way, and to balance these feelings with feelings of love and esteem for others. So there is no way one can monitor the final, desperate outburst of destructive rage that one has set oneself up to have.

The Compliant Christian

The *manipulative pattern* of being a Compliant Christian begins when the child learns that he or she can win the approval of parents or others by *pleasing* and *placating*. The child mistakes getting their approval for being loved. So we can say that he or she becomes stuck on the *love* polarity. The problem is that in getting the approval of others, one makes everyone else the judge and master. Therefore, one must constantly repress feelings of strength or anger, and instead feel only love and weakness. One fears that if one expresses rights, strength, or power, others will withdraw their approval and retaliate with rejection or abandonment. What one does not see is that in living up to everyone else's expectations and demands, one sacrifices one's own individuality and originality.

Without the rhythms of anger and strength, the compliant Christian is easily taken advantage of by others. Of course, he or she allows this to happen over and over again because of the fear of expressing anger or irritation. This person is like a "crying doormat," who invites people to step on him or her—then feels miserable and abused when they do!

Because Compliant Christians are unable to stand up to others, or even to say no or disagree with them, their love loses its genuineness. The love that they could have degenerates into a sticky, parasitic dependence. The body type reflects dependence, as the muscles are underdeveloped and flaccid.

61

THE COMPLIANT CHRISTIAN

The price of constantly living the "nice guy" or "nice girl" role is fatigue, resentment, and inner emptiness. Also, in living one's life to gain other people's approval, one's God-given identity remains undeveloped. The payoff for such a life-style is the occasional crumb of approval or pat on the head that one receives for being so nice to others.

At the *character level,* the pleasing and placating pattern degenerates to overt *dependence.* Now the person denies all personal power and responsibility for shaping his or her life and becomes a clinging vine around someone else's life. One constantly looks to the other person for what to feel, what to say, where to go, what to believe, ad infinitum. This person feels that if the other person dies or leaves he or she will be completely lost and helpless. Many popular songs reflect this misguided approach to love with such lyrics as "without you I would be nothing." Unfortunately, this exaggerated sense of dependence might be true, but it certainly is not a virtuous trait. It means that one is neurotically dependent and incapable of feeling, thinking, and choosing for oneself. Many unhappy marriages are made by one partner's being overly dominant and the other's becoming excessively compliant and dependent.

Because of our cultural standards, Christian women especially seem to fall into the compliant trap. They are taught as little girls that their sole mission in life is to grow up, have a family, and take care of a husband and children. What they are not given is a healthy dose of self-esteem so that they are deeply attuned to their own wants, needs, desires, talents, and gifts. So life becomes slavery as they become frantically busy, self-sacrificing, and often desperately lonely.

The fallacy of the compliant syndrome is that one erases oneself in order to "love" others. But the Bible—as well as good psychology—says clearly to love others *as* ourselves; that is, to be as concerned about our own growth and well-being as we are about theirs. It also means developing a healthy *inter*dependence in relationships as opposed to the desperate dependence of the compliant person. The concept of healthy interdependence will be explored more fully in chapter 12.

In its *psychotic form,* the compliant life-style gives way to *depression*. Somehow it creeps into the awareness of the person that he or she is nothing but an empty hull. All the beliefs, values, feelings, and opinions that one has belong to someone else. One has completely lost touch with one's inner being.

Psychotic depression is the result of years of constricting the inner rhythm of feelings. The final result is immobility and paralysis. The depression reflects the psychological reality of always being pressed down by the demands, desires, and expectations of others. The person finally loses hope and becomes numb. Even the body takes on a sagging and down-in-the-mouth appearance over the years. The face may feign a smile on the surface, but the evidence that deep sorrow and loneliness are underneath is shown by the wrinkles in the brow, eyes, and at the corner of the mouth.

Since the Compliant Christian long ago lost touch with his or her own dignity, anger, and power, the years of being everyone's slave have now taken their toll. The psyche collapses under the one last demand that is finally too much. The ultimate, tragic expression of psychotic depression is suicide.

Mary is a middle-aged housewife with whom Dan worked in counseling over a period of two years. The settings ranged from an in-patient psychiatric unit to a growth-oriented church group. During the two years, Mary made excellent progress in moving from apathy and self-hate to a position of active and caring involvement in life. Although Mary made three suicide attempts during the two years, a combination of prayer and effective psychotherapy finally enabled her to learn to stand on her own feet, take responsibility for her own life, tell others how she really felt about things, and regain faith for living an interesting and fulfilling life. Mary has now reentered family, church, and community life with far more awareness and skills for coping than she had ever thought possible.

Mary's life shows once again that it is possible to reverse even the most vicious patterns of self-destruction. Of course, it is always best to discover destructive patterns in one's life long before they bear bitter fruit.

Perhaps the reader will be able to apply insights gained in the study of this chapter to enjoy greater self-awareness and understanding of others.

Summary

In order to facilitate an overview of the deterioration process presented in this chapter, we here present Figure 3: Process of Deterioration. Notice that the center of the figure is fear.

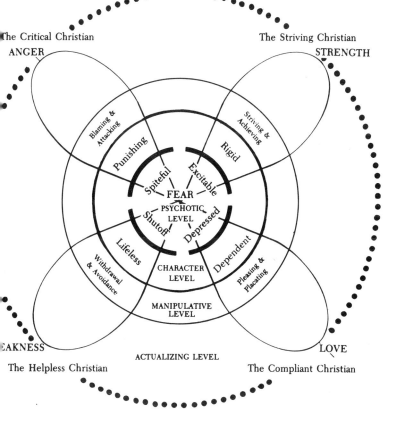

Figure 3: PROCESS OF DETERIORATION

It is sometimes quite sobering to realize that, whatever else hell is, it is certainly the brutal process of dehumanization that eventually leaves a person numb, rigid, alone, disoriented, and shut up. In the deterioration to various levels of manipulation, character disorder, and psychosis, we see a separation from one's God-given invitation to actualization and a descent into the abyss of hell.

Everyone is a mixture of manipulative styles and character types. We live within the context of a fallen and twisted reality. The "mystery of iniquity" is passed on from generation to generation. It contaminates culture, education, politics, economics, religion, and the sophisticated social systems of this world.

Defenses are learned strategies; we are not born with them. Once we discover how we make ourselves tense, rigid, and controlled in our posture toward life, we can begin to reverse the process. That is at once the burden of responsibility and the potential for joy for all human beings. There is light at the end of the tunnel! There is hope for the troubled, entangled, and imprisoned individual. Our faith in the creative grace that will lead us to wholeness is warranted.

But the process of growing out of our psychological ruts is not without risk and pain. We may have to experience the real travail of owning our feelings and learning to express them honestly to others before we begin to enjoy the celebration of restored meaning in our lives.

Every way of being stuck can be understood as an overt or subtle *distortion* of man's existential calling: to love himself, others, and God wholeheartedly.

This is where it becomes important to realize that praying about our life situation must be combined with the courage to *do* something about it. Otherwise our "prayers" are only a form of avoidance—a flight into fantasy and magical thinking. God may truly inspire us along the wisest pathway for our lives, but we must take the responsibility for doing the walking or we will never get anywhere. And if we take a wrong turn, we must have courage to back up and try a new pathway.

A strong feeling of fear, anxiety, hostility, guilt, or depression may be a signpost that indicates that one has gotten off the track. If one becomes aware of these feelings, and exercises the courage to look for new and different options, then growth can be restored and one is back on the path of healthy living again. The fruits of that direction will also be felt in the personality as peace, joy, and excitement.

No one has escaped developing certain nonactualizing or manipulative patterns. But an awareness of how these patterns are being acted out in one's life creates the possibility of experimentation with new alternatives, growth, and change. This possibility is the hope of the actualizing Christian. It is the invitation of Christ to each individual, and the joy of a God who delights in giving good things to those who seek him. It is also the finest meaning of salvation, redemption, and the grace of God.

6. The Healing Power of Love

To trust God is to be enabled to trust oneself at the very core of one's being. . . . Once we have been grasped by God's affirmation of us, we have experienced love at the very heart of things, a love that cannot and will not let us go. And the power of that love begins to make all things in this fragmented world whole again.
—Theodore Runyon

We have seen how a person's God-given actualizing tendencies can be thwarted—how authentic responses to life can deteriorate into manipulative patterns, then into character styles, and finally, into psychotic conditions. The process could be visualized as in Figure 4, as an ever-constricting downward spiral of fear that squeezes out of a human life the God-inspired call to greatness.

The other side of human experience, also shown in Figure 4, is the *upward* spiral of *expansion.* In this process, a person begins to manifest individual greatness by operating more and more in an actualizing way from his or her core. We will explore this process of expansion and actualizing in the remainder of the book.

Our central thesis is that *perfect love casts out fear* (I John 4:18 RSV). This healing love causes the joyful expansion rather than the fearful constriction of the human personality. The Greek word that is used in the New Testament for this perfect love is *agape.* This could be translated as spontaneous,

68

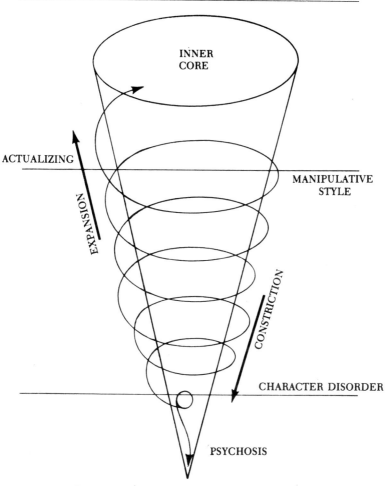

Figure 4: EXPANSION VERSUS CONSTRICTION

altruistic love that involves unselfishly willing the highest good of another. It is a love that cherishes, affirms, and respects the uniqueness of another person. When we say in religious language that "underneath are the everlasting arms," we are symbolizing the agape dimension of love that God has for every person and that is to be experienced in one's core.

Psychiatrist Viktor Frankl has written eloquently about this kind of love and the growth-enhancing effects it has in the life of the beloved.

> Love is the only way to grasp another human being in the innermost core of his personality. No one can become fully aware of the very essence of another human being unless he loves him. By the spiritual act of love he is enabled to see the essential traits and features of the beloved person; and even more he sees that which is potential in him. Furthermore, by his love, the loving person enables the beloved person to actualize these potentialities. By making him aware of what he can be and of what he should become he makes these potentialities come true. (*Man's Search for Meaning,* p. 113)

It is being in contact with unresolved fear at the center of the personality that results in the manipulative styles of living that we have examined. But *when we feel deeply loved, understood, and accepted in the core of our being, then our fears are healed changes and we find ourselves on the road to actualizing.* As Thomas Merton has said:

> Our ability to be sincere with ourselves, with God, and with other men is really proportionate to our capacity for sincere love. And the sincerity of our love depends in large measure upon our capacity to believe ourselves loved. Most of the moral and mental and even religious complexities of our time go back to our desperate fear that we are not and can never be really loved by anyone. (*No Man Is an Island,* p. 201)

Whether or not one feels loved by God, one is. So a basic step in actualizing is to trust that, whether or not one understands it, one is deeply loved and affirmed by God in the core of one's being.

To nurture an awareness of this perfect love may have different connotations for the Christian as opposed to the non-Christian. The Christian who goes through life becoming increasingly aware of the pure and intimate love that God has for him or her, has faith that the process of sanctification or growing in Christlikeness is inevitable. The Christian would probably think of this in terms of new fruits continually being born in his or her personality and relationships. In Galatians, Paul lists these fruits as "love, joy, peace, patience, kindness, goodness, faithfulness, gentleness, self-control" (5:22, 23 RSV).

For the non-Christian, much the same process may be unfolding although one is not really aware of growing also by the grace of God. In one's openness to the truth about one's life, one can experience a clarification of one's life situation, a deep trust in one's own being, and a growing sense of relatedness to the universe. The healing love God has for mankind, and the love that people can experience for one another, is the spiritual birthright of every human being.

Being affirmed by love at the core of one's being, the actualizing person does not need to waste energy proving, defending, controlling, or abusing oneself. One is set free to *be* oneself in a caring and respectful way, and to *express* oneself to others and to God in ways that are spontaneous, sincere, and creative. Being grounded in the fertile soil of God's love, one is free to grow.

God's loving us perfectly does not guarantee that we will always *feel* loved. The sun always shines on the earth, but sometimes a cloud blocks out the warmth that the earth receives. So it is with the growing Christian. There are times of oasis, and there are times of desert. There are times of ecstatic awareness of God's presence, and there are times when one's prayers seem to bounce off the ceiling. But for the actualizing Christian, even pain, frustration, confusion, and struggle are inspired tutors. In one's heart, one learns to say with Christ, "Not my will, but thine be done," and with Job, "Though he slay me, yet will I trust in him."

So the actualizing life is based on more than just good times or good feelings. It is based on the courage to know the truth about oneself and one's destiny. This is why faith is at the heart of the Christian life-style. Only faith can be open to God's sovereignty whatever the circumstances may be. Faith can penetrate the mystery of God's love even when human understanding is darkened.

To change from manipulating to actualizing does not require that one become something different from what one is. It simply means living more and more from one's core being, which is infused in the most intimate way with God's creative Spirit.

To actualize is to unfold in our core being like a flower in bloom. The petals are like the four primary polarities described throughout this book. The process occurs in God's good time if we are open to it.

Again, referring to Figure 4, when on the actualizing pathway, a person moves into an ever-expanding sphere of meaningful and intimate relationships. This can happen as we receive more and more of the nourishment of God's healing love. As life progresses, we become more vibrant, feeling-ful, and alive. The inner core is constantly enlarged throughout our being. Our sense of connectedness to God, nature, and mankind increases throughout life.

The Gift of the Spirit

We can experience God's love in a very direct and intimate way. This comes about through a spiritual relationship with Jesus Christ, and through the presence of the Holy Spirit, the gift that Jesus asked God to give us. As Jesus said to his disciples,

> And I will pray the Father, and he will give you another Counselor, to be with you for ever, even the Spirit of truth, whom the world cannot receive, because it neither sees him nor knows him; you know him, for he dwells with you, and will be in you. (John 14:16-18 RSV)

The Holy Spirit bears witness that we are the sons and daughters of God (Romans 8:16). The Spirit is the Comforter, the Counselor. We may seem too far away from Christ to have a personal relationship with him, but the Holy Spirit can bring us together with him. The gift of the Holy Spirit is that which helps us to know, in an intimate way, God's love.

We realize that this concept of the Holy Spirit may not have much meaning for some of you who are oriented primarily to psychology rather than religion. Consider with us the possibility that the Holy Spirit—this mysterious energy that may be difficult to understand—is the personal Presence and source of inspiration for growth and fulfillment among human beings. Even some of our Christian readers may have difficulty accepting this premise, because the Holy Spirit has sometimes been viewed as the vague third member of the Trinity who is spoken of in the Apostles' Creed but not experienced directly in daily life. But the Holy Spirit can give us the comfort and the power to live life openly in love, not in a fearful hiding place. "For God hath not given us the spirit of fear; but of power, and of love, and of a sound mind" (II Timothy 1:7 RSV).

The Holy Spirit can be understood to come from within the personality much as a seed is placed within fertile soil. It is like a mustard seed that grows gradually from within, as opposed to a mustard-plaster which is slapped on from without.

We like the understanding that theologian Theodore Runyon brings to this issue:

> Because God values and respects our human freedom, the presence of His Spirit may be ignored or overlooked or buried beneath years of insensitivity and indifference. . . . Jesus never imposes himself on anyone. He meticulously honors the right of people to turn away from him as well as toward him, because his reign is not something that can be imposed but must be freely willed by anyone who would be his follower. (*What the Spirit Is Saying to the Churches*, p. 14)

Thus, the first step of the person who would know Christ is simply to become aware that he is already "closer than breathing, nearer than hands and feet." Second, the person must surrender to his will for one's life, learning daily to seek the guidance of the Holy Spirit that enables one to fulfill his will.

Some Christians believe that wholeness will happen

automatically as soon as they come into a personal relationship with Jesus Christ. We wish to point out that one of the mysteries of the Christian faith is that while one has the peace of Jesus' being close at hand, one is still in a creative tension. This is because we are in a *process* of growing. That is, Christianity affirms that the kingdom of God is at hand; yet at the same time it has not yet fully come. The Holy Spirit is in the world and in the personality of the Christian; yet the Christian is still not a perfectly loving and wise being. As Billy Graham has said, being born again does not mean that "we will never have any problems. This is not true, but we do have Someone to help us face our problems. The Christian life is not a way 'out' but a way 'through' life" *(How to Be Born Again).*

The Holy Spirit wants to form in and through our lives a unique expression of our Christlikeness. That expression takes into account every dimension of our lives—genetic and physical makeup, metabolic and hormonal systems, emotionality, experiences in the environment, place in culture and history, special calling and destiny, and our unique relationship with Jesus Christ in this life and in life eternal.

It is striking in this context to note that the Greek word used in the New Testament to characterize the activity of the Holy Spirit in the human personality is *dynamis.* This probably looks familiar to the reader because it is the root word out of which our words for dynamo and dynamite have evolved. So when Christ tells his disciples (Acts 1:8) that they shall receive *power (dynamis)* when the Holy Spirit comes upon them, he is saying that a dynamic new presence of energy will flow into their lives. The process of an outward flow of vitality and energy from the depths of the personality is the very opposite dynamic of the kind of collapsing inward of the personality that we have called deterioration.

The actualizing Christian is moved in his or her core being by the presence and power of the Holy Spirit. Instead of tending toward spiritual and psychological deadness, one is continually animated and inspired by the Holy Spirit. The ironclad chains

74

of fear are broken, and the Spirit guides one along the wisest pathway for one's life.

At the core level a profound experience occurs again and again in the life of the growing Christian. The Holy Spirit moves rhythmically and reliably back and forth within one's day-to-day awareness. Just as the ocean tides move in and out, so does the Holy Spirit move now into the foreground of awareness, now into the background, but always near at hand. The result is that through all the experiences of life, the person still feels loved in his or her core. *The power of love is that it heals our fears and inspires our greatness.*

We have simply to come out of our hiding places, surrender to the love of God, and receive his gift of the Holy Spirit to guide our lives.

The Actualizing Process

In this chapter, we wish to examine Figure 5, the Process of Actualizing. You can see that this figure is similar to Figure 3 (chapter 5, page 65).

But notice immediately that *perfect love* has replaced fear at the center. And the core at the center has expanded more, as we showed in Figure 4 (chapter 6, page 69).

In the process of actualizing, one expresses oneself less on the character and manipulative levels and moves more into the actualizing expressions of each polarity. For instance, on the strength polarity, one may express oneself once in awhile in a rigid manner. Occasionally, one may employ manipulative tactics of striving and achieving. But mostly one learns to express strength in an actualizing manner, by being powerful, strong, capable, or adequate as it is appropriate. If one were actualiz*ed,* one would express only the actualizing level. But we are in a process, and this is why we need to be aware that our manipulative tendencies can be only gradually neutralized.

The best model for understanding the actualizing life is Jesus himself. Jesus possessed a quality of being that awed people wherever he went. In his encounters with others, he would

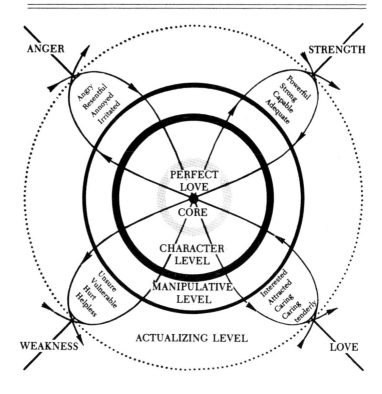

Figure 5: THE PROCESS OF ACTUALIZING

leave healing, change, and renewal. He lived from his core and was able to express the intensity of emotion required for every situation. He could be *loving* enough to restore and free a woman caught in the act of adultery when her accusers wanted to stone her to death. He could be *angry* enough to make a whip and physically drive the money changers from the temple. He could be *weak* enough to surrender to being put to death on a cross and buried in another man's tomb. He could be *strong* enough to rise from the grave a victor over death itself.

Knowing that God participates with one in the quest for authenticity and meaningful involvement in the world brings courage to trust the subtle promptings of one's inner feelings or to be open to the wisdom of one's gut reactions. The actualizing Christian values the still, quiet voice *within* that often reflects the gentle guidance of the Holy Spirit in the core of one's personality.

Inputs from God and others flow readily through the permeable boundary of the self and on into the core. We can describe the process as dynamic and continuous. Persons who live this way are being maximally sensitive to themselves and others. They function transparently: what originates deep within is what is expressed honestly to others. They are also moved emotionally by the feelings that other people share. Thus we could say these persons are congruent and empathetic.

An important aspect of growth is having the courage to accept our losses up to now. A woman once shared in a counseling session with Ev how tragic she thought it was that certain insights had come so late in life. He reassured her that it was a blessing that the insights had come at all. Now the issue was to take the insights and build on them.

The fact is that life is not just a rose garden—it can be a crown of thorns as well. So we must learn to accept our losses and defeats and get on with the adventure of living.

In giving up our radical defenses and bags of tricks, we are reborn. We become like babes, lovable to behold. We experience the freshness, purity, and genuineness that are truly Christlike. But we do not become naïve and simplistic. Rather, we grow to be as Jesus said, "wise as serpents and innocent as doves" (Matthew 10:16 RSV).

As we give in to spontaneous expression from our core along the primary polarities, integration gradually takes place and inner harmony is experienced. This process takes time, just as building up a pattern of repressing feelings took time. The actualizing response must be made again and again before it becomes an automatic expression of our core being.

Also, the transformation from manipulating into actualizing involves a fundamental change of attitude toward self and others. Notice that the arrows in Figure 5 move outward to go with *ex*pression of the self, rather than with the ulterior motives of *im*pressing others or *re*pressing one's feeling. One chooses to *ap*proach and encounter others—even when the going gets rough—rather than *re*proach or avoid them. Further, the arrows also point *inward*. The Holy Spirit flows *into* the depths of the Christian just as it did for Christ. This is important to know, because it assures us that our whole being—physical, emotional, and psychological—is the ground out of which emerges the unfolding will of God in our lives, as it did in Jesus' life.

All the essential elements for an actualizing life-style are already in the personality. Nothing needs to be added or taken away. We simply work, with God's help, to restore the inner balance so that we can live with more integrity.

With awareness, patience, and gentle discipline, the patterns of character styles become stages of growth—like the bud that eventually gives way to the blossoming of the flower. Gentleness is an important concept here. If someone impatiently tried to tear the covering of the bud away, the flower inside would be destroyed. In the same way, we need to be respectful of slow and gradual transformation of the constricted personality into the fully alive and expressive one.

With courage the actualizing Christian recognizes within himself or herself the possibility for deterioration into psychosis, or growth into Spirit-led actualization. It is this potentiality for psychosis or actualizing that makes each day a creative act of personal surrender to the miracle of God's abiding grace.

Rollo May writes:

> The transformation from neurosis to personality health is indeed a wonderful process. The person rises on the force of hope out of the depths of his despair. His cowardice is replaced by courage. The rigid bonds of his selfishness are broken down by a taste of the gratification of unselfishness. Joy wells up and streams over his pain. And love comes into the man's life to vanquish his loneliness. He has at last found himself—and found his fellow men and his place in the universe. Such is the transformation from neurosis to personality health. And such is

78

what it means, likewise, to experience religion. (*The Art of Counseling,* pp. 223-24)

The Bible is clear that the kingdom of God need not begin only when one goes to heaven. Rather, the kingdom of God has already burst into time and space and history (Ladd, *A Theology of the New Testament*). The more we live from our cores, the more we experience the gracious powers of the kingdom of God—here and now. So the actualizing Christian has hope not only for a blessed eternity but also for substantial healing, meaning, and fulfillment in *this* life (Schaeffer, *True Spirituality*).

Many Christians are not sufficiently aware of this exciting prospect. An example is a marine sergeant who was recently talking to Dan. He confided sincerely that he was afraid to make a deep commitment to Christ because he felt he could not handle the new obligation to straighten out his life and give up some bad habits he enjoyed. "If I surrender to God, he will judge me and send me to some remote corner of earth," he said. Dan suggested that the whole meaning of the death and resurrection of Christ was that God loves each one of us perfectly. So why would a loving God want to make Jim miserable? God sent Jesus into the world to liberate people, not to condemn and frustrate them. Jim had never seen that side of it, but had rather assumed that God was the kind of gruff and stern Being with whom one ought not to get too intimate—a punitive God. But this is simply not true. God is *for* us, not against us!

Given the balance of *desire* to be all that we are called by God to be, *courage* to be ourselves here and now, and *openness* to grow day by day, we cannot help making the metamorphosis from caterpillar to butterfly.

One Person's Experience in Growing

Elizabeth, a student in several of Dan's psychology classes, is experiencing firsthand the pain and joy of growing. In her late thirties, having just added a third child to her family, she felt an

79

urge to begin a college education. This brought into her awareness some painful issues of identity, role confusion, and reponsibility to self and others. After a year of pursuing a new direction in her life, she wrote the following:

Whoever was the first to make the analogy between caterpillars and butterflies and death and resurrection—old life and new life—must have had a "butterfly experience." And to a certain degree, so have I.

Knots being untied; tight jar lids being loosened—it is freedom. It is freeing. It is the slow motion experience of leaping through a meadow with arms and legs in tune with the rhythm of life. But somehow the butterfly says it best, because of the cocoon experience.

People seem to have more than one go-round with the cocoon. How did it start for me this time? Why did it start?

I was happy as a caterpillar. Just a bit confined, that is all. I viewed myself, and others did, as fuzzy-wuzzy, problem free, happily married, financially secure, basking in the love of God . . . but I was not content.

I did not know myself. Actually, I did not even know that I did not know myself. And I certainly did not own my feelings. I had to move away from all those who unknowingly kept me as a pet caterpillar to learn the true situation. And that is why I ended up here at college.

Things have happened fast, which I like. But it has been a difficult, thrilling, laborious, joyous, arduous, and climactic year. There have been so many significant encounters. Every week of classes I have learned so much. But several things were of major importance.

Almost a passing comment by Dr. Montgomery turned a trickle into a flood last fall when he said, "Liz, I sense a lot of tension in you—and have since we first met." I could hardly believe it. Everybody knew how calm, cool, and collected I always was. I was not tense . . . how could he say that?

I was only going to school full time, keeping my husband happy, preparing three meals a day, cleaning the house, taking my son to Cub Scouts and piano lessons, taking my daughter to Brownies and ice skating, and giving constant attention to my new baby girl! Tense . . . tense! How true! I had to face it. And so began a whole chain of discoveries.

I thought I was relaxed and learned myself I was tense. I thought I was well-adjusted and learned that I did not even know myself. I thought I was loving and learned that I was often indifferent. I thought I was social and learned that I was withdrawn. On the positive side, I thought I was dumb and learned I was intelligent.

At an earlier point in my Christian life, it would have seemed unspiritual to consider these things. But somewhere near the beginning of this year, I experienced a glorious assurance that God was in fact the One who had led me to this point—and he was leading me through!

For some reason, it seems that it is almost over. Or maybe it is the beginning of a new era building on what I have learned. I do know that I am more excited about life. I love my husband and children more than ever before. And I am more open to forming friendships with new people I meet. Most of all, I feel more comfortable being myself. In this year of growth I have come in touch with my own worth and potential.

Simply becoming aware was a great part of the answer. Perhaps that is because I wanted the change. I really do want to be a transparent person.

For now all I can say is that something deep is happening within me—and I love what is happening.

7. All You're Meant to Be

Man alone, of all the creatures of the earth, can change his own pattern. Man alone is the architect of his destiny. The greatest discovery of our generation is that human beings, by changing the inner attitudes of their minds, can change the outer aspects of their lives.

—*William James*

It has been found (Carl Rogers, Abraham Maslow) that as people become more psychologically healthy (fully functioning, self-actualizing) they become more tolerant of "opposites" within themselves, and become more able to accept others with all their uniqueness. Rogers describes this as an increasing "openness to experience" *(On Becoming a Person).*

Christians often think in terms of opposites—right/wrong, good/bad, sinfulness/goodness—instead of the principle of *transcendence of opposites*. The actualizing Christian learns to transcend these opposites. Openness to experience *all* that one is can be expressed as follows:

I am neither good nor bad, I am both.
I am neither spiritual nor sensual, I am both.
I am neither generous nor selfish, I am both.
I am neither honest nor dishonest, I am both.
I am neither a saint nor a sinner, I am both.

82

But God accepts me, forgives me, and loves me just as
I am.
    And I can accept, forgive, and love myself and others.
            (Osborne, *The Art of Learning to Love Yourself*)

The testimony of the actualizing Christian is not that he or
she is perfect, but rather that he or she is *being perfected* by the
healing love and power of God. The process of being made
whole involves gradual transformation of one's entire being.
    In Figure 6 we wish to show actualizing ways in which the
polarities of strength/weakness, love/anger can be expressed.
Every polarity has both manipulative and actualizing alternatives. To be consistently actualizing, a person must learn to
transform manipulative behaviors into actualizing counterparts. The transformation process is the focus of chapters 8
through 11.
    On the strength polarity, the egocentric manipulative tactics of
striving and *achieving* need to be transformed into the
interpersonal qualities of *cooperating* and *contributing*. The
latter two actualizing qualities have a respect and sensitivity that
the manipulative forms do not possess. Cooperating with others
in a sharing way allows us to express our own strengths while at
the same time seeking the common good. Contributing is not
something that is grasped at or forced, but rather is a reflection of
our true capabilities. Our attitude becomes cooperative rather
than competitive. We give up the attempt to be omniscient and
omnipotent. When we function in this way, we do not feel
threatened by someone else's contributions or accomplishments.
We are also quick to admit our deficiencies and to integrate our
strengths with the contributions of others. This is the basis for the
virtue of courage or realistic self-confidence.
    On the weakness polarity, *withdrawing* and *avoiding* need to
be transformed into *feeling vulnerable* and *empathizing*. The
actualizing Christian learns that he or she can honestly share
feelings of inadequacy, fear, or helplessness. In sharing feelings
of vulnerability, a person becomes more accepting and tolerant
of others, and hence more empathetic. Herein lies the *virtue of
humility*.

83

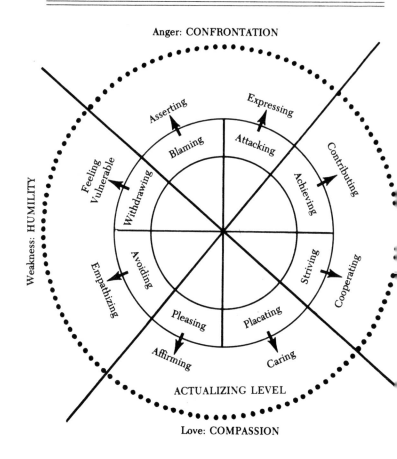

Figure 6: ACTUALIZING ALTERNATIVES TO MANIPULATING

Author's personal comment—Ev:
Some years ago my mother went back home to Sweden for the first time in thirty years. Late one night we received a concerned phone call from her during which she said that the Gripsholm, *the boat she was supposed to return on, had*

collided in New York Harbor with the Andrea Dorea, *an Italian ship. We discussed her alternatives, and it seemed the only thing she could do would be to take her first airplane trip. This may not seem like a large accomplishment these days, but for my mother, who was over seventy years old, this was a fearful and difficult task.*

The next day she bravely climbed the steps of the huge 707, turned the corner, and sat down in her seat—which happened to be next to Eleanor Roosevelt! Eleanor Roosevelt was an empathetic woman who herself had suffered much in her life. So immediately her empathy expressed itself to my mother, who obviously was somewhat shaken at being on her first plane trip. The worldly, yet gentle woman pulled a rose from the bouquet the Swedish government had given her on departure—and gave it to my mother. Mother was deeply moved by this gesture and immediately felt vulnerable and open to this beautifully warm woman. During the next five hours on their journey to America, the two of them chatted together like neighbors over the back fence, as my mother often did with her friends in Rockford, Illinois.

Eleanor Roosevelt is an example of a truly humble person. Since she was genuinely aware of her own feelings of vulnerability, she could reach out to others, including my mother, with a special warmth and sensitivity.

On the love polarity, the manipulative patterns of *pleasing* and *placating* are transformed into the actualizing traits of *affirming* and *caring*. There is a freedom to praise and nurture both oneself and others. Built into the combination of affirming and caring are firmness and warmth. From these qualities emerge the *virtue of compassion,* a sure mark of the actualizing Christian.

From the anger polarity arise *asserting* and *expressing,* the actualizing counterparts of *blaming* and *attacking*. The person who expresses anger graciously and diplomatically exhibits the *virtue of confrontation* with caring, or "speaking the truth in love."

There is a real wisdom built into the warp and woof of human nature. It is as though God intended a sensitive set of checks and balances in order to create a reliable source of guidance and inspiration within each person.

Love that is expressed fully brings qualities of tenderness, caring, and nurturing into the world. However, to find its finest balance, love must be offset with a certain firmness and power that is captured in the feeling of anger. Anger provides the energy for confronting the world in a caring way.

Likewise, the feelings of strength and weakness both balance and check each other. From strength a person derives a certain air of confidence, boldness, and dignity. But with the balancing effect of weakness, the virtue of humility is added; so one can express strength in gentle and humble ways.

It is our belief that as one becomes more balanced in expressing these behavioral opposites, one will experience a connectedness to others and to God in a warmhearted, open, and sharing way. Connectedness is the key to understanding others and growing with them in mutually supportive ways.

8. Owning Strengths

Be not afraid of greatness: some are born great, some achieve greatness, and some have greatness thrust upon them.
—William Shakespeare

Jonah the Old Testament prophet had the same problem of many modern-day Christians: he ran away from his own great calling.

The nonactualizing Christian may not be swallowed by a whale, but probably God will arrange some modern kind of encounter that will awaken us to our greatness and unique mission in life.

Jesus showed the ability to jar people into an awareness of their potential for fulfillment. According to the Gospel narratives, Jesus moved prostitutes, tax collectors, religious workers, fishermen, shepherds, soldiers—anyone. Ironically, in surrendering to personal encounter with Jesus, they discovered how valuable and great they themselves were!

Yet in the church today, there are often messages given to people that say: "Don't think too highly of yourself"; "There is nothing great about you; only God is great"; "Pride goes before the fall." This can lead to a false sense of humility or even a self-hatred.

The individual who has difficulty accepting his or her

genuine and God-given strengths often discounts compliments instead of graciously receiving and appreciating them. He or she probably has difficulty complimenting or praising others too.

The Scriptures present a different picture of the believer. Just as God gives his glory to Christ, Jesus gives his glory to the Christian (John 17:22). The actualizing Christian discovers this and feels gratitude, strength, and joy. As in Figure 7, one can verbalize one's feelings by such phrases as "I am adequate," "I am capable," "I am strong," and "I am powerful." The awareness of one's strengths, gifts, and talents is an important part of healthy self-love and self-esteem.

The actualizing alternative to an overbearing strength is personal power. When one does not need to use absolute control over others or oneself, but rather feels that he or she is a vessel through which the power of the Holy Spirit is expressed, then one can say with Paul: "It is no longer I who live, but Christ who lives in me" (Galatians 2:20 RSV). When this happens, relationships cease to be authoritarian, controlling, or manipulative, but rather emphasize cooperation and give maximum space to be.

Sensing one's strengths is reflected in an unpretentious kind of self-confidence. Because the actualizing Christian's strength is rooted in the grace of God, one shares in God's serenity. The Psalmist expresses it this way: "He is like a tree planted by streams of water, that yields its fruit in its season, and its leaf does not wither. In all that he does, he prospers" (Psalm 1:3 RSV). This is not the manipulative form of strength that we saw in chapter 5; the Striving Christian was rigid, tense, and compulsive. Rather, this genuine type of strength is a quiet, relaxed flow of power from the presence of the Holy Spirit in one's life. The actualizing Christian can do great things in the world, but the way that these things are done does not come across to others as arrogant, self-conscious, or forced. The actualizing Christian experiences firsthand the biblical principle, "'Not by might nor by power, but by my Spirit,' says the Lord" (Zechariah 4:6 RSV).

88

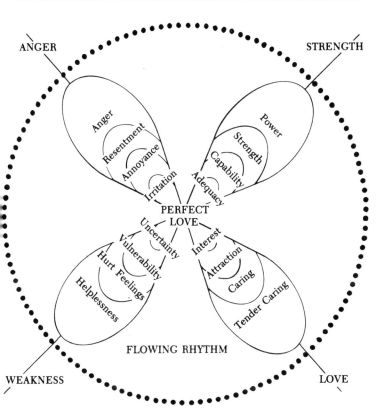

ANGER

STRENGTH

Anger

Resentment

Annoyance

Irritation

Power

Strength

Capability

Adequacy

PERFECT
LOVE

Uncertainty

Vulnerability

Hurt Feelings

Helplessness

Interest

Attraction

Caring

Tender Caring

FLOWING RHYTHM

WEAKNESS

LOVE

Figure 7: THE ACTUALIZING SPECTRUM

Intellectually, the actualizing Christian is committed to the principle that to experience, or to be, the feeling of strength is commendable and is not an expression of conceit. The person therefore enjoys and even savors feelings of security, adequacy, and worth.

The peaceful sense of strength and self-confidence that

emerges from being aware of one's own worth and uniqueness is vital for effective living. Dave is a Christian who is struggling to understand the real meaning of personal strength. He strove desperately, especially with peers where he works, to prove to everyone how adequate he was. He tried to do more work in less time than anyone else. His real motives tended to surface during the lunch hour, when everyone paused for a quick volleyball game. Dave's mood for the rest of the day depended upon whether or not his team won the game. If they won, his ego was bolstered and he felt exuberant. If they lost, he became irritable and depressed. On days that he lost, his wife and children became recipients of all his negative feelings when he got home.

What Dave has learned through participating in a church growth group is that there is a deeper, more reliable source of personal worth and adequacy available to him. It is the love of God, the love and respect that others have for him, and his own ability to value himself positively. As this sinks in more and more, Dave is becoming increasingly consistent in feeling adequate and worthy throughout the day—regardless of how much work is done or whether his volleyball team wins or loses. He is becoming freer to approach both his work and his relationships in a creative rather than a competitive way. This is the actualizing expression of the strength polarity. Dave is learning to transform *striving* and *achieving* into *contributing* and *cooperating*.

Emotionally, the actualizing person is committed to the expression of inner strength, not as an attempt to experience power over others, but rather as an expression of the potency of his or her own being. The person who knows how to experience and express strength in an actualizing way is a real asset to any relationship of which he or she is a part. For instance, in friendship, marriage, work or community life, this person can be relied upon to be fresh and original. Because the person is not bound by false modesty, there will be a continual flow of creative contributions that come from deep within. These qualities make the person inwardly attractive and interesting.

This reflects both how the person experiences life and how other people tend to experience the person who is realistically in good contact with the strength polarity of personality.

A key to the healthy expression of strength for the actualizing person is that the personal power that is experienced is used not only in behalf of his or her own well-being, but also as a service to facilitate the well-being and happiness of others. Thus the power of the actualizing Christian is used to edify or build up others, rather than to dominate, intimidate, or exploit them. It is a power made gentle by Christ's love and insulated by the virtue of humility.

Bodily, the strength dimension is experienced by a sense of being able to stand on one's own two feet and by the ability to reach out and ask for what one wants. We have found that people who are out of touch with the strength polarity can to some extent begin to discover it by stamping their feet firmly into the ground. This exercise provides a real sense of the feeling of one's own *strength,* for the lower half of the body is where people get their support. If one *stamps one's feet* firmly into the ground until one feels the muscle strain in calves and thighs, one's feet will seem to become firmly planted in the ground, like the roots of a tree. This helps one feel a sense of strength and self-support.

A second exercise, helpful for developing strong resistance to manipulation from one's environment is to lie on a bed with both knees up and to pound the bed with both fists and say, "I won't give up! I can do it!" Both movement and voice should express conviction.

Some practical ways that one's strengths might be expressed in everyday living are as follows:

* ★ participating equally in conversations
* ★ taking initiative in greeting or meeting others
* ★ giving and receiving genuine compliments
* ★ giving and receiving constructive criticism
* ★ speaking up and negotiating for your reasonable rights
* ★ speaking out for the reasonable rights of others

* using expressive talk to show feelings
* being able to say yes or no when necessary
* being willing to confront and handle stressful situations

This may seem like a formidable list for people who are not used to experiencing or expressing their strength. However, it is important to have these behaviors as part of one's total repertoire of possibilities for interacting with others. These skills can be learned with patience and practice. As Ralph Waldo Emerson has said, "A great part of courage is having done the thing before."

One further characteristic of strength is that it enables us to become active participants in life. When we are in touch with our strength, we don't sit around and gripe, complain, or whine. We do something. We take responsibility for shaping our own lives and the world around us. We may pray with St. Francis of Assisi: "Lord, help me to accept the things I cannot change, and *change the things that I can*. And give me wisdom to know the difference."

9. Surrendering to Weakness

It is the laden bough that hangs low, and the most fruitful Christian who is the most humble.

—Anonymous

In American culture, there is a taboo against vulnerability, especially for men. Seldom can we allow ourselves such phrases as "I am unsure," "I feel vulnerable," "I feel hurt," or "I feel helpless." (See Figure 7.) And yet we all have these feelings from time to time. We all feel anxious, scared, helpless, or weak.

In our culture, where competition, individuality, and performance reign supreme, it is no surprise that any sense of weakness is repressed from awareness. Yet, when a part of us that is quite real is pushed out of consciousness, we are more vulnerable than ever because we lose touch with our core being. Then our energies are diverted into presenting a false self to the world. We even believe that this ideal self—secure, flawless, and capable in all situations—is our real self. This kind of vanity is the real target of the scriptural "pride goeth before destruction" (Proverbs 16:18).

Author's personal comment—Ev:
John was a patient of mine for almost a year. He was a real example of the macho type of person—suave, debonair, charming with the women, and always in control.

In group therapy his chauvinistic attitudes would often cause women to feel hurt and angry. But until his experience in therapy, he had just always assumed that women were inferior to men, and that men always had to be strong and fearless.

One of the exercises that I tried with John had good results. I knew that he was stuck on the strength and anger polarities and that somehow we needed to mobilize his sense of weakness and tenderness. So I had him lean with his back against the wall, feet spread shoulder width, and begin gradually to lower himself toward the floor. This position puts the body under real stress, since the person is fighting gravity and must eventually give in to weakness. This was exactly what John needed to experience.

As he was slowly sinking to the floor, I encouraged him to let out the feelings of pain that he felt. He could hardly do it, because he had learned as a kid to act tough. After several times of going through the exercise, he began to let out loud moans and groans, even letting his body shake and tremble under the stress.

What John began to learn was that it was all right to experience and express his pain and weakness. At first he had been terribly embarrassed. But he came to be more accepting of his limitations. He was even able to cry freely for the first time in his life.

When John reentered the group, he was able to be more relaxed. If he felt hurt, he cried. If he felt angry, he would say so. And if he felt tenderness, he would risk expressing it to someone. Everyone in the group noticed the changes in John's life over the weeks. The tenseness was turning to mellowness. The need to manipulate and control others, especially women, was changing to a desire to communicate honestly. And the courage to accept his weaknesses proved a doorway to experiencing real self-esteem.

I had another patient, Bill, who had a similar insight, but this time it had to do with God. In one particular session, Bill seemed to have reached the end of the line. He had lost all hope for meaning in his life and for a good relationship with his wife.

Moved by intuition, I decided to ask him to engage in an exercise that would help him surrender to his sense of weakness.

He leaned his back and hips on my outstretched arms and hands as he gradually fell to the floor. He struggled to resist falling, yet realized that no human effort could hold him up permanently. Ever so gradually, we both fell to the floor, coming into contact with the "ground" for support.

As he finally sank to the floor, a deep peace enveloped him, for he experienced himself surrendering to God—in the sense of God as the Ground of Being. He shared that although he had been an agnostic for many years, this powerful experience enabled him to get in touch with a power greater than himself, the Supreme Being.

God is far more accepting of our real weaknesses than most of us realize. As the Psalmist said: "As a father has compassion on his children, so has the Lord compassion on all who fear him. For he knows our frame; he remembers that we are dust" (Psalm 103:13-14 NEB). It is in owning our weaknesses that we have access to the presence of God. He welcomes those who confess their need. And the greatest need is for communion with God. In the New Testament both James and Peter reiterate the Old Testament theme: "God is opposed to the proud, but gives grace to the humble" (James 4:6; I Peter 5:5 NASB).

If we desire to encounter and surrender to God, we must become aware of our helplessness. We must experience the reality that on our own, if apart from God's plan and resources, we will live a partial and fragmented life. This is why the Bible, from Genesis through Revelation, emphasizes that God meets face to face with those of a humble heart, while resisting people who are rigid and controlling in their arrogance.

But here we must make a distinction between humbling ourselves, on the one hand, and becoming helpless, servile, and self-effacing, on the other. While the Scriptures advocate a certain *childlike* openness and honesty in relating to God and

95

others, they do not teach us to remain fixated at a *childish* level of development. This is what the Helpless Christian does not understand. So he or she gets stuck at the infantile stage of psychological and spiritual development. But in order to restore the rhythm of growth, the manipulative tactics of *withdrawing* and *avoiding* need to be transformed into the actualizing qualities of *feeling vulnerable* and *empathizing*.

As pointed out earlier, in the account of Eleanor Roosevelt, getting in touch with one's own helplessness, pain, and vulnerability is an excellent way to develop the quality of empathy toward others. This particular quality, expressed at its finest in Jesus, made him so approachable by the common people and by little children.

The actualizing Christian seeks to integrate the childlike qualities of openness to experience, freshness of perception, and excitement in living, with the more adult qualities of awareness of the consequences of one's behavior and discipline in expressing oneself. Thus the actualizing Christian is free to keep growing and maturing, while at the same time preserving and giving the finest expression to the feelings of vulnerability and childlike spontaneity. This is the dynamic out of which the virtue of humility emerges. One remains humbly reliant upon God concerning every dimension of one's life; yet one takes responsibility to face life and live it to the fullest. Every time one feels overwhelmed by life, one's feeling of vulnerability is an occasion to draw near to God or to a trusted friend for comfort, guidance, and courage. The old Christian hymn by Charlotte Elliott seems to say it well:

> Just as I am, without one plea,
> But that thy blood was shed for me,
> And that thou bidst me come to thee,
> O Lamb of God, I come, I come!
>
> Just as I am, though tossed about
> With many a conflict, many a doubt,
> Fightings and fears within, without,
> O Lamb of God, I come, I come!

Author's personal comment—Dan:

In my relationship with my wife, Tammie, I have had to learn how to express my weaknesses and fears openly. This has not been easy, because I sometimes have the appearance of being like the Rock of Gibraltar. Recently I had a very difficult week involving many demands on my time and energy. One night it all caught up with me. I lay in bed feeling overwhelmed by all that was happening. As I began to get in touch with my feelings I started trembling. I was feeling frightened, helpless, and alone.

Tammie sensed that I was feeling upset and asked me to share my feelings with her. I crawled into her arms, much like a frightened child, and told her my fears as she cuddled me. Her love and tenderness were so reassuring that my feelings of vulnerability began to be transformed into feelings of confidence and courage. I fell asleep in her arms, and experienced a profound peace the rest of the night.

The actualizing Christian must learn to experience directly the hurts of life. There are many little hurts that we may experience from day to day that are real and painful. A sharp word from one's spouse, a disappointment over a shattered hope, or an unfortunate misunderstanding with a friend might generate inner feelings of hurt. If these feelings are not allowed into awareness, we might become irritable, restless, or depressed later in the day. As we become aware in a particular moment that we feel hurt, we seek to find a way to handle it. We may confront the person who has caused the hurt and honestly share our hurt feelings with the other person. Or we may decide that our skin is too thin and we need to be a little more realistic in letting people's criticisms or insults bounce off. Or we might share the feelings of hurt with a trusted friend.

The experience of hurt and vulnerability can also lead us to the Lord, who himself experienced persecution, misunderstanding, and betrayal. Paul was well acquainted with this process, for he wrote: "For the sake of Christ, . . . I am content with weaknesses, insults, hardships, persecutions, and calamities; for when I am weak, then I am strong" (II Corinthians 12:10 RSV). In Christ we find a Friend who empathizes with our deepest hurt and, with his understanding, restores hope to our lives.

Out of accepting hurt and experiencing pain, the actualizing Christian emerges from the situation with dignity and strength intact. The deep and lasting Source of one's dignity is not man, but God. We know that to be dependent on the approval and praise of everyone is to make everyone our judge. If that were the source of our dignity, we would have precious little of it in this life because people tend to make heavy demands upon those whom they praise. Feeling loved and affirmed by God, we experience new courage to continue the adventure of living. A student of Dan's once wrote:

> For a long time I blocked off feelings of hurt, but now I realize that hurting and loving are both aspects of experiencing life. If you want to experience love you must also be open to the possibility of experiencing pain. I am also learning how to separate the feelings of everyday ups and downs from the steady love and peace I get from God.

A more profound expression of hurt and vulnerability is grief. Grief is experienced when a person experiences a loss that seems to strike the core of one's being. This is captured well by the word "brokenhearted." Perhaps an intimate relationship has abruptly ended. Perhaps there has been an accident that has destroyed one's property or one's health. Perhaps a dear friend has moved away. Or perhaps someone has died—a parent, spouse, child, or friend.

In the solitude of grieving, one needs to find courage to trust one's God-given emotional and physiological processes that allow for full and honest expression of inner pain—crying, moaning, trembling, or shaking. One of the unfortunate ways that this natural healing process is blocked is by responding to the cultural message that says crying is a sign of weakness. The message implies that one should bear hurt with grim resignation. We believe this to be destructive and false.

98

Anne Morrow Lindbergh has described beautifully the importance of vulnerability in being human:

> Grief is the great leveler. . . . Stoicism . . . is only a halfway house. . . . It is a shield, permissible for a short time only. In the end one has to discard shields and remain open and vulnerable. Otherwise, scar tissue will seal off the wound and no growth will follow. To grow, to be reborn, one must remain vulnerable—open to love but also hideously open to the possibility of more suffering. (*Hour of Gold, Hour of Lead,* p. 215)

If the natural grieving process is blocked, then there can be no psychological "closure" about the situation. The psychological wound cannot heal. The feelings may eventually be repressed or "forgotten," but the pressure remains because the body musculature is literally locked into place for weeks, months, or even years. Therefore, the face remains tense, the breathing continues to be shallow and guarded, and the body posture is frozen in a stiff, corpselike manner. How unlike Christ himself, who, when he felt sorrow and pain, wept openly (John 11:35).

If a person is to get back into touch with life, he or she must give in to the profound feelings of hurt and pain as the flood of emotional energy is discharged. When we can give vent to hurt feelings, we are able to see things in a new way. We can finally accept what has happened, take the losses realistically, and move on. Having had the courage to give up a fanatical hold on how things "should have been," we now are able to regain touch with events, relationships, and circumstances that are currently emerging in our lives. In this way we gain *closure* on the situation, and it recedes into the background of our awareness. We are now free to live again, in the present! Thus, we become excited about living because we rediscover the rich possibilities for actualizing here and now.

10. Expressing Love

They are the true disciples of Christ, not who know most, but who love most.

—Frederich Spanheim the Elder

The love end of the anger/love polarity is expressed verbally with phrases such as "I'm interested," "I'm attracted," "I care," and "I care tenderly." (See Figure 7.) The actualizing Christian has access to the experience and effective expression of these several intensities of love.

Loving tenderness is a need all people have, and yet in American culture such expression is often discouraged. Grace Stuart explains in a passage from *Narcissus:*

> It is too seldom mentioned that the baby, being quite small for quite a long time, is a handled creature, handled and held. The touch of hands on the body is one of the first and last of physical experiences and we deeply need that it be tender. We want to touch . . . and a culture that has placed a taboo on tenderness leaves us stroking our dogs and cats when we may not stroke each other. We want to be touched . . . and often we dare not say so. . . . We are starved for the laying on of hands.

Christian psychiatrist Paul Tournier, in *A Place for You,* has emphasized that one must first receive before one has anything to give. If one has not received tender and affectionate feelings from parents, friends, or the Lord, then it is understandable that one may have difficulty dealing with these feelings. It is one thing to "know" in one's head that one is loved; it is another thing to "feel" it in one's heart. Most of us have been damaged to some extent by well-intentioned parents who firmly believed they loved us, yet did not know how to effectively communicate that love through cuddling, praise, and affirmation.

Dorothy Law Nolte has eloquently expressed the effect of love that is *felt* in the life of a child. What she says applies to adults as well.

> If a child lives with encouragement,
>   He learns confidence.

> If a child lives with praise,
>   He learns to appreciate.

> If a child lives with fairness,
>   He learns justice.

> If a child lives with security,
>   He learns to have faith.

> If a child lives with approval,
>   He learns to like himself.

> If a child lives with acceptance and friendship,
>   He learns to find love in the world.

All of the foregoing lends credence to the idea that, in *experiencing* love developmentally, people also *learn* to love. It is in being loved that one learns to love. But sometimes the very deprivation of love in growing up can become a strong motivator in learning how to go about giving and receiving love as an adult. The person who has not been adequately loved can become especially sensitive to the need for love in the world. Not taking love for granted, this person may grow substantially in his or her lifetime in the ability to love self and others.

It seems possible, then, that both satisfaction and deprivation of one's needs to feel loved and appreciated can become tutors in the art of learning to love. It is not simply what happens developmentally that determines one's personhood, but rather what one does about it through awareness and choice. It is self-knowledge, facilitated by the presence of the Holy Spirit in one's life, that enables one to discover needs and wants and to make them known in the loving relationships of later years. This provides a second chance to actualize oneself in becoming a sensitive and loving human being.

Psychiatrist Karl Menninger, in *Love Against Hate,* has said that human beings really *do* want to love one another but just do not know how to go about it. The actualizing Christian learns to accept responsibility for finding out how to get the flow of love going in his or her own life. Even though one's need for feeling loved may never be fully met in this life, one can go a long way toward learning to love oneself, feeling God's love, and daring to risk loving others. Here again the quotation, "Underneath are the everlasting arms," has meaning.

Author's personal comment—Dan:
I once taught a class in human values. One of the deepest values that kept cropping up was love.

One day when we were talking about love, I sensed a peculiar tension and uneasiness in Sally. I asked her if she would like to add anything to what we had been saying. She flushed and replied that, although she had been a Christian ever since she could remember, she had never felt lovable. Somehow she had gotten the idea that she was a depraved, ugly, and unlovable person. She reported that she knew in her head that God and others loved her, but she had managed to insulate herself from ever experiencing directly her "lovability" and "loveliness." In fact, she had developed a habit of discounting people's compliments and erasing from her mind positive feedback that she received.

I invited Sally to sit in the middle of the circle the class formed. Then I looked her straight in the eye and told her that I felt love for her. Gradually, other members of the class began to share their positive and caring feelings for her. Some even got up from their seats and walked over to hug her. She felt

102

*overwhelmed—at first with embarrassment, then with joy.
Tears streamed down her face.*

*I sensed that there was another way of expanding the
awareness that was dawning on her. I had her stand up on her
chair and say: "I am lovable." At first she said it very timidly,
and the class got after her for discounting herself again. Again
and again she tried saying it. Then somehow she began to
experience firsthand the real meaning of what she was saying.
She stood up straighter, took a deep breath, and shouted: "I am
lovable!" Again and again she shouted it with tears welling
down her face. When she got back down, the whole class
cheered and applauded. Many in the class reported that they,
too, had never felt as much in touch with the power of being
loved as they had in those moments.*

*Many weeks later Sally told the class that her "lovability"
experience had been a turning point for her. Now she was
becoming more aware of her worth, her rights, and her
potential for a fulfilling life.*

We must have security in being ourselves and in feeling
significant and worthwhile before we will dare to reach and
touch the world in a caring way. This has the effect of providing
us with a sense of power out of which we can choose to love.
Thus, we can put away the childish manipulations of *pleasing*
and *placating* (the Compliant Christian discussed in chapter 5)
and take up the more actualizing forms of love: *affirming* and
caring.

When we begin to learn how to love our selves, we discover
that we have new energy and courage to reach out in love to
others. And, paradoxically, love can only be kept when it is
given freely to others.

To describe the principle that love can only be kept by being
given away, we use the following analogy. In Palestine there are
two bodies of water connected by the Jordan River: the Lake of
Galilee and the Dead Sea. There is a vast difference between
the two.

The Lake of Galilee is rich in its supply of fish. In New

Testament times, it was the scene of Christ's calling of several of the disciples who were fishermen by trade. The Lake of Galilee both receives its supply of water from, and returns water to, the Jordan River. Therefore, the water is always fresh and clean, and the lake not only supports marine life but also provides food for human life outside its boundaries.

After the Jordan River leaves the Lake of Galilee, it enters the Dead Sea some sixty miles southward. However, the Dead Sea is so far below sea level that it has no outlet; the water evaporates, leaving a high concentration of salts, which kills all fish in its depths and makes it unfit for human consumption. Its waters, by being constantly held within its boundaries, become bitter, stagnant, and brackish. And so it is with the person who only receives from others and from life, and refuses to give freely out of what he or she has received.

One of the things that most blocks the flowing of love back and forth in relationships is one-upmanship. By this, we mean that one or both persons have a need to win or always be right. This is especially prevalent in marriage relationships, where it takes a high toll in casualties. But it also occurs in all other relationships.

Most of us have heard the manipulative guidelines for establishing controlling relationships with others: "Never show your real feelings to others if you want to keep them interested"; "Play hard to get"; "Use put-downs to keep the other person in place"; "Always keep the other person guessing"; or "Try to wrap them around your finger." These messages reflect a profound lack of awareness about what makes for healthy, enjoyable, mutually enriching relationships.

If these messages have played a part in molding our personality, then they will probably still be contaminating our present relationships with spouse, children, friends, or fellow workers. Thus, we may continue to exploit and manipulate others to satisfy our unconscious drive for power, security, and control. We will use others in a way that reveals *loveless power,* not the *power of love,* to be the root of our existence.

What is needed is the ability and insight to change

relationships from a power struggle to a mutually beneficial exchange. Rollo May defines such love as a "delight in the presence of the other person and an affirming of his or her value and development as much as one's own" *(Man's Search for Himself)*. Paul emphasizes similar qualities in his famous passage on love found in I Corinthians 13. He writes that "love is patient and kind; love is not jealous or boastful; it is not arrogant or rude. . . . It . . . rejoices in the right" (RSV). Love has the rare ability to be pleased rather than threatened by the talents, achievements, and triumphs of others.

An important principle for people, especially married couples, to realize is that God often moves through their closest relationships to teach them more and more about themselves and about life. Therefore, the wise person learns to value the honest and loving feedback that those closest to him or her are able to provide. This changes the format of a relationship from a struggle for power to an opportunity for growth and enrichment. The persons become partners, each committed both to his or her own deepest fulfillment *and* to the highest good of the other.

The experience of companionship and the expression of caring are essential ingredients for living life fully. Abraham Lincoln said that "the better part of one's life consists of one's friendships." When someone cares, it is easier to work, to play, to speak, and to listen. When someone cares, it is easier to find meaning in life.

It will help us greatly along the journey toward wholeness if we can develop friendships based on honesty, trust, and love. An anonymous author once wrote:

> Friendship is the comfort of feeling safe with a person, having neither to weigh thoughts nor measure words, but pouring all—right out—just as they are, chaff and grain together, certain that a faithful friendly hand will take and sift them, keep what is worth keeping and, with a breath of comfort, blow the rest away.

The relationship of love is the most effective way of bridging the unbridgeable gap between two separate human beings. To feel truly loved—that is, deeply accepted and understood by another person or by God—is liberating. It enables one to be seen in the context of one's weaknesses, faults, and psychological or physical shortcomings. Such behaviors as pretending to be what one is not, defending oneself, or striving to attract or impress the other person gradually fall away. They are replaced by a growing honesty and spontaneity in self-expression and a greater feeling of being natural in the relationship. This leads to the paradox that the more one surrenders in a genuinely loving relationship, the more one becomes one's true self. The more one gives to the other, the more one receives.

Jesus expressed this principle when he taught people to develop a *giving attitude:* "Give, and it will be given to you; good measure, pressed down, shaken together, running over, will be put into your lap. For the measure you give [*to others*] will be the measure you get back" (Luke 6:38 RSV).

The Christian life-style can be summed up in the one word—"love." Outgoing love that results in concrete deeds of service is the fruit of one who is being led by the Holy Spirit.

Touching other people's lives in a caring way can take many forms. One may develop the awareness to often compliment, praise, and admire one's spouse and children. One may learn to be gracious in relating to colleagues, employer, or employees. One may offer service to a stranger in need. One may practice being considerate in daily transactions with others in such diverse activities as shopping, handling business, or driving on the freeway.

As growing persons, we can give ourselves permission to try out new behavior. We can *experiment* in daily transactions with others by expressing a smile, a warm greeting, a pleasant compliment, or a gentle touch. Before long, there will be greater coordination of our feelings, thoughts, and bodily actions. As a feeling of compassion stirs us, we can caringly touch people and tell them of our concern. When a feeling of admiration emerges, we can tell people how much we appreciate them and perhaps touch their hands or shoulders as we do so. If we feel joy with others, we might hug them or clasp their hands. If we feel playful, we might want to joke or physically jostle with them.

These options and many more can become sincere, effective ways to communicate our positive feelings to others. Of course, any of these channels can be reduced to the level of manipulative tactics. That is why the actualizing Christian develops the paradoxical qualities of prudent openness, discriminating trust, and disciplined spontaneity in the expression of his or her love to others.

The Scriptures teach that compassion and caring ought to be extended to all human beings, above and beyond our normal sphere of relationships. The Christian is called to experience an ever-widening sphere of meaningful personal relationships throughout life. There is no age limit to this. But courage is required at any age to reach out to others and to risk sharing their joys and their sorrows. This does not mean that we ought to distress ourselves terribly about other people's misfortunes. But it does indicate that we ought to nurture an attitude of profound respect for the well-being of others and that we should give sincerely what we can in terms of time, energy, and financial and material resources to meet some of the needs of a suffering humanity. Jesus expresses his profound identification with the suffering of mankind when he says: "I was naked and you clothed me, I was sick and you visited me, I was in prison and you came to me" (Matthew 25:36 RSV). And James adds that "Religion that is pure and undefiled before God and the Father is this: to visit orphans and widows in their affliction" (James 1:27 RSV).

As actualizing Christians, we do not insulate ourselves from suffering in the world. We instead become vessels through which the love of God can flow to bring comfort to the brokenhearted, impart courage to those who are losing hope, and creatively seek to meet needs as they arise in people's lives.

Loving involves a choice and therefore may be rightly understood as being an act of will. This implies a sense of duty in

107

the loving relationship, "in sickness and in health, for better or for worse." A truly loving relationship is not a flighty or transitory affair. It is a trustworthy commitment that endures even in the face of hardship or sacrifice. It is a faithful caring that *actively* seeks the well-being and fulfillment of the beloved.

In loving, we are most like Jesus and most truly ourselves.

11. Asserting Anger

Anger in a relationship is like salt in a meal. Too little leaves things drab and tasteless. Too much poisons. But a pinch now and then makes for a savory friendship.

—*Dan Montgomery*

All people feel angry from time to time. It is a natural and important feeling. But many Christians have been conditioned to see anger as an undesirable response. And it is true that anger can be expressed in manipulative ways. The Critical Christian uses anger to manipulate self and others. He or she is stuck on the anger polarity. What the Critical Christian and all of us need to learn is how to deal with our anger in actualizing ways.

One can choose to express oneself angrily most of the time or one may choose never to express one's anger, but it usually comes out in some manner.

Anger that is not sufficiently acknowledged or expressed creates an unfinished situation within. The repressed anger then comes out in indirect and unconscious ways. For instance, the man who gets mad at his boss, but keeps smiling in order not to make waves, may go home and yell at his wife over some trivial event. The wife may then displace her anger onto the children, who may in their turn kick the dog. All this displacement causes confusion, hurt feelings, and no constructive gain of awareness for anyone. Beside this, the original unresolved situation with the boss will not change magically. Rather it will fester like a painful sore.

In feeling angry toward another person, one should first seek within oneself for the source of the irritation and communicate honestly with oneself about the cause. Then, if it would be constructive, one can find some way to honestly let the other person know so that the person can take the feeling into account. Otherwise, the other person is left in the dark, and the relationship may turn sour. It is for this reason that Paul writes: "If you are angry, don't sin by nursing your grudge. Don't let the sun go down with you still angry—get it over quickly" (Ephesians 4:26 TLB). Paul encourages the Christian to learn how to speak the truth in love (Ephesians 4:15).

For the actualizing Christian, anger is expressed as responsible assertion. It reflects sensitivity to oneself and others. It involves learning to stand on one's own feet and take up for oneself or others when it is appropriate to do so.

The point most people miss regarding anger is that our anger is a part of *us*. It does not belong to the other person in the sense that the other person created our anger. Our anger is our response to that person's behavior. The expression of anger would be much more constructive if people remembered this and did not blame others for their anger.

The seed of truth in why many Christians have not wanted to express their anger is valid: expressing one's anger manipulatively as blaming or attacking is destructive. As Paul says, "Let all bitterness and wrath . . . be put away from you, with all malice" (Ephesians 4:31 RSV).

One needs to learn to express anger constructively. A basic guideline is to *assert* and *express* oneself rather than to *blame* and *attack* the other person.

For instance, in the cartoon in chapter 5 about the Critical Christian, we quoted this person (Sam) as saying, "Why are you so stupid?" He has already made an assumption that the other person (John) is stupid. This results in an attacking form of anger.

A healthier way of dealing with this anger would be for Sam

first to recognize that he feels angry that John is "stupid." He moves now to his feeling, not the fact, that John is stupid. Now Sam has alternatives for understanding his anger.

If Sam truly listens, he can have a *dialogue with his core*. (This is the principle Maslow meant when he referred to one's "inner Supreme Court.") Simply by asking himself inwardly, Sam may get the answer from his core that "you are angry because the bank teller this morning treated you as if you were stupid." Sam can then realize that because he did not deal with his anger then, he is now projecting his anger on John—calling him stupid, when in reality he is angry at the bank teller.

Or, Sam may get the answer from his core that he is upset because the project he and John are working on together is more important to Sam than he had realized and now John is not fulfilling his share of the work. In this case, Sam needs to take the time to examine whether he thinks John is capable. If he is capable, Sam may now decide that he needs to express to John that his not fulfilling his share of the work is delaying the project.

If Sam realizes that John just cannot do the job, he may let him go and bring in someone else. Blaming John for his inability at this point would not be actualizing; but, expressing to him that he is not showing the needed skills, and that that is why he is being let go, would be actualizing.

Many answers come quickly from the core—the preceding possibilities could surface in seconds. The more we listen to our cores, the more we hear—and know how to listen. Sometimes, though, we ask and do not hear an answer. Or we get what we think is an answer and then proceed to act on it—and make things worse.

Remember that becoming actualizing is a process. If we were perfectly actualized now, the answers would always be there crystal clear and our behavior would be "perfect." As we are in a process of becoming actualizing, sometimes we do the most effective thing and sometimes we make mistakes. Mistakes are just that—"miss-takes." Our lives become most meaningful when we live from our own core, finding our own truest answers. So it is a process worth living—and the mistakes are worth making. The real key here is not to blame and attack ourselves for those miss-takes, but to keep learning with more "takes." Having patience with ourselves often makes it easier to become more patient and forgiving of others. It can sometimes relieve our anger just to remember that other people are in the growing process, too, and not always taking what to us would seem the most effective action.

As actualizing Christians, we seek to do the will of God. Doing his will involves having good will toward others and ourselves. We do this by listening to our anger, taking it to our core, and then responding from our core. Anger can only become actualizing if one deals with it by expressing and asserting it, rather than blaming and attacking someone. Blaming and attacking are simply manipulative, whereas expressing and asserting include a quality of genuine respect for everyone involved.

In communicating our anger honestly, we get it off our chests, and the rhythm of life is reestablished. We finish with it and move on to experience a new and different feeling.

The range of feelings in the anger polarity, as shown in Figure 7, page 89, includes irritation, annoyance, resentment, and anger. The intensity of the feeling increases as one passes from irritation to anger.

Recognizing irritation, boredom, or annoyance at the lower levels of intensity within the anger spectrum enables us to avoid unwittingly building up to levels of resentment, hostility, and hatred. In handling these feelings, it is important to learn to acknowledge the mild forms and deal with them on a "cash and carry" basis. That way we don't save them up like coupons to be redeemed in one sudden, destructive explosion.

While our anger may sometimes reach intensities approaching hatred, we need never go so far as to write a person off completely. It is really possible to have compassion for and pray for our enemies—that God in his mercy might help them through their own dilemmas, frustrations, and pains. Yet, we can be honest about the effects on us of their behavior.

112

Many Christians who are afraid to verbalize their feelings of anger fear that if any form of anger is let out, it will result in destructive behavior. But the person who can give honest vent early to his or her angry feelings need not fear violence. On the contrary, the "nice guys" who never let themselves get angry are the ones who may end up harming others. All Christians need occasional "hostilectomies."

In associating the expression of anger only with the most intense expressions of roughness, explosiveness, or physical violence, we may have never considered how to express our anger in more gracious and considerate ways. The expression of anger in a relationship does not have to lead to a permanent breach or to a bitter rejection. Rather, it can lead toward greater mutual respect and sensitivity to one another. Communicating our anger in an actualizing way can also clear the air of phoniness.

Priest-psychologist Adrian van Kaam has suggested that when we feel angry we must not smile sweetly or freeze sullenly. We need to learn instead to be humble and courageous enough before God to let our feelings come out—straight, honest, and simple, yet wisely and not destructively.

We might simply say: "I am feeling angry (or hurt) about what you just said (or did). Here is the meaning it has for me . . ." Then we let the other person express his or her feelings and perceptions. In this way we remain open to each other, yet preserve our spiritual and emotional integrity by expressing what we feel.

If it does not seem wise to express our feelings directly in a particular situation, then we might discharge the feeling with full awareness at a later time and place. For instance we might:

★ talk to a trusted friend about the incident
★ write down our feelings on a piece of paper
★ run around the block
★ beat up a pillow
★ find a safe place and scream

★ go for a vigorous swim
★ tell God how angry we are, as the psalmist David often did.

Author's personal comment—Dan:
I learned much about the importance of anger by working with a student and counselee named Sharon. Sharon is an attractive, popular young woman who was raised in a pastor's family. Over the years she had embraced the Christian way of life and experienced a devoted and loving relationship with Christ.

However, another pattern had also developed over the years. As a child she had gotten the idea that serving God meant completely denying herself and putting all of her energies into meeting everyone else's needs. Unfortunately, many people took advantage of her desire to serve by making all kinds of demands on her. As she grew up she became everyone's puppet, with hardly a private moment to herself. She was pushed and pulled by those around her.

During a counseling session, I asked her to take out a lifetime of resentment and anger by beating on a pillow. She became timid and said that she was not mad at anyone. So I got up and stood over her, placed my hands on her shoulders, pushed down firmly, and began reciting all the demands that people had laid on her. "Do this for me!" I shouted. "Oh, Sharon, you simply must lead this Bible study." "Sharon, you have to speak in church this Sunday." "You have to sing a song for us next week!" "You must help me out by doing this job for me." "You just have to take care of this problem for me!" And on and on.

At first she just smiled and took it. Then her eyes became tearful. I continued verbally making demands and physically putting pressure on her shoulders. Finally, I saw a flash of anger in her eyes. That anger had always been there, but she was only now getting in touch with it.

Suddenly she pushed my hands off her shoulders, stood up, and told me she wasn't going to do another thing for such a tyrant. She shouted that she had rights too, and feelings! I placed the pillow in front of her and told her to get out some of

114

the angry feeling. Very slowly at first, then with great enthusiasm, she pounded the pillow and called off a series of about ten names of people who had used and exploited her over the years. Finally, as she finished discharging the reservoir of anger, she heaved a sigh of relief and smiled.

"I did not know I was so mad," she said as she laughed. "Boy, I finally got to tell those people how I really felt. I don't think I am going to let people push me into a corner like that anymore. I love people, but they don't have a right to take advantage of me. I have my rights too!"

I watched Sharon take this new awareness into her life over the next two years. She is finding the balance that she longed for through the extra dimension of firmness and dignity in her personality.

What is often important in this process, as in Sharon's case, is that we convert the energy behind the feeling into verbal or muscular activity (Lowen, *Bioenergetics*). Anger, when given full and satisfying actualizing expression, is followed by a sense of relief, peace, and muscular relaxation. We are now open to a variety of other feelings. One of the first is often a feeling of warmth and love for the very person with whom we have been angry.

In studying the life of Jesus, we find several occasions when he expressed his anger toward his own disciples. He showed how he felt when they misunderstood him, quarreled with one another, kept children away from him, or tempted him to go against the will of the Father. By the same token, he never left them in doubt about his lasting gentle care.

Jesus expressed more intense levels of anger and rage against the Pharisees and those who were adept at manipulative devices and phoniness. Yet his prayer at his death demonstrated that forgiving love, not accumulated bitterness, had nourished the roots of his personality throughout life: "Father, forgive them . . ."

Anger, rightly expressed, serves the ends of love and justice in our lives.

12. The Christian Walk

There are many in the Church as well as out of it who need to learn that Christianity is neither a creed nor a ceremonial, but a life vitally connected with a loving Christ.

—*Josiah Strong*

We believe that the primary teaching of Jesus Christ was not a fear-motivated message. Rather, Jesus moved people when he spoke of love, gentleness, and blessedness. We feel that the alternative to a fear-oriented religion is a religion based on free will and love. Emphasis on love stresses that Christ must be freely chosen. Too often, Christ is presented in the context of damnation and hell, and the convert becomes the object of fearful coercion.

Psychology has shown time and again that fear is not a permanent motivator. The example of Hitler and of other dictators has shown that people are temporarily motivated by fear, but in the long run, motivation based on love is much more trustworthy and permanent.

Furthermore, the constriction that fear causes keeps us from living freely in the here and now. All expression of the polarities is reduced and constricted when one stays in fear at the center of one's being. When fear is diminished or absent, one can contact a *pure* place within, where one can truly experience the love of Christ. As Paul wrote, "There is therefore now no condemnation for those who are in Christ Jesus" (Romans 8:1 RSV). We describe this pure place as the core, and thus our emphasis on the importance of learning to contact it.

We see the Christian journey as marked by two phases: first, the initial decision, and then the long journey that lasts the rest of one's life. The initial experience does not make one perfect. It is just the beginning. As someone has said, "We have to walk the walk, not simply talk the talk." The rest of one's life becomes a process by which one becomes more and more perfectly loving as Christ himself is loving.

One becomes an actualizing Christian by living within the guidelines of Christ's perfect love and not by fearfully trying to please God or others.

The dove is one of the biblical symbols for the Holy Spirit, because the Spirit reveals his wisdom and love through gentleness like that of the dove. It does not facilitate the quiet and gradual work of the Spirit in our lives if we approach growth in a tense, legalistic, and tight-jawed way. The psychological equivalent of this is introspectionism.

When an integration of principles of psychology is attempted for a fuller understanding of religious life, the temptation is to make the psychology a new law, a new burden to be borne by the Christian.

The point of the Christian life is to *live fully and joyfully,* not to dwell in a self-absorbed and overcritical way on our perceived faults or virtues. As Irenaeus said in the second century, "The Glory of God is a human being who is fully alive!"

The power of the gospel is that Christ has come and the kingdom of God has burst in upon us. The powers of the kingdom of God are being released from the core depths of our being. Even now, the Spirit is at work within our core, guiding us in daily transformation to ever greater approximations of Christlikeness. It remains a work of grace, not a reflection of strife and effort on our part. Van Kaam, in *Woman at the Well,* writes:

> We are empty vessels to be filled by the Lord. To be filled with the life of Jesus in accordance with who we deeply are is the

117

Christian definition of self fulfillment. . . . We will see in eternal gratefulness how the inner spring of grace made our deepest self similar to Jesus. We will see how the spring inside us leaps with dazzling splendor for all eternity.

The Bible calls the Presence of the Holy Spirit in our lives an earnest, or pledge or down payment, on the full unrestrained Presence of God that we will eventually know. In Ephesians, Paul speaks of this earnest: "You . . . were sealed with the promised Holy Spirit, which is the guarantee of our inheritance until we acquire possession of it, to the praise of his glory" (1:13, 14 RSV). Substantial fruit will be born from our consistent trust in the Holy Spirit in this life. And in Galatians, Paul develops a description of the fruit of the Spirit that can be seen emerging from fertile union of the believer with Christ: "The fruit of the Spirit is love, joy, peace, patience, kindness, goodness, faithfulness, gentleness, self-control; against such things there is no law" (5:22, 23 RSV).

So the actualizing Christian is saved from the heavy burdens of both fear and self-conscious introspection by the larger context in which he or she understands life. One feels grounded in God's unshakable and enduring love. We know that our faults, sins, and rigidities do not make us less acceptable to God, who only wants us to shed the things that would oppress us and take up the things that will bless us.

Many people have lost contact with the spiritual core of their being. They no longer trust the inspired impulses from within. Instead, they take orders from their surroundings—from the media, from the authority figures, from peers, from economic pressures, from fads, or from gurus. There are instances, of course, when tradition, authority, society, or an enlightened teacher can aid the individual in beneficial ways. However, following the mentality of the crowd and the ways of the world often leads to spiritual deadness and deterioration of the personality.

In coming home to the core, one gives up one's defensive style of living, which has been based on fear, manipulation, and pretense. One adopts instead a growth-oriented life-style based on love, trust, and genuineness. *Perfect love* replaces fear as the motivating dynamic of one's life.

As we have already pointed out, this process is often slow and gradual, for fear is a tenacious guest who is reluctant to be ousted. But given time, even in harsh conditions, the God-inspired personality will still bring forth its bloom in due season. This is a tribute to both the resourcefulness of God and the openness of the person.

The challenge of genuine religious commitment in the Hebrew-Christian sense is to be transformed, to be made whole, to "*taste* and *see* that the Lord is good" (Psalm 34:8 RSV). The process of being moved toward wholeness and authenticity by the inner power of the Holy Spirit is a lifelong adventure.

Actualizing, for both the devoted Christian and the modern secular person, involves learning to rediscover, affirm, and trust the sacred ground of Being within. As Bonhoeffer has expressed in *Ethics,* it is a coming home to one's Origin. It is slipping into the tailor-made clothing of one's original spiritual calling. In our words, it is accepting God's gracious invitation to actualize one's full potential.

Effortless Effort

The challenge of living from one's core involves "effortless effort." The paradox is that the harder one tries, the more one fails. It is like learning to swim: the more you struggle to stay on the surface, the faster you go under. On the other hand, the more you relax, the easier it becomes to float.

Living has to do with surrendering versus forcing. The key, then, is learning to live spontaneously rather than by coercion and willpower. It involves learning to live without striving. And this is contrary to what we in Western culture have been taught: that we win by trying harder.

Another example is trying to make someone love you. The more you try, the less you succeed. You can never force anyone to love you. You can only be yourself openly, and hope that he or she will choose to respond to you.

But many people take the other course of trying to force or

trick others into loving them through their achievements, seductions, or bag of manipulative tricks. All who perpetually strive to merit love end up exhausted and alone. Love cannot be bought or earned. It is the free gift of all who develop a relaxed and caring presence to others, and arises spontaneously out of heartfelt human encounter.

In an age of technology such as ours, it may be difficult to accept that some things—such as wisdom, the capacity to love, the courage to be oneself, and the sensitivity to actualize one's spiritual destiny—cannot be reduced to a prefabricated "instant" package.

One of the paradoxical aspects of personal growth is that it can never be forced. An invitation can be given, but the person must grow at his or her own pace. It is important to realize that one cannot force one's own growth! Rather, one must have time, patience, and willingness for growth to occur at its own rate.

The paradox of growth within the human personality is that we grow and change by accepting the way we are. We grow most when we relax. The reason for this is that relaxed awareness, coupled with desire, allows our whole being time to digest and assimilate new experiences and subsequently alter our thoughts, feelings, values, and behavior.

A wise philosopher once said that human beings are like sheep. If they truly assimilate their experiences, then gradually the grass of daily life will be transformed into the wool of wisdom.

When it comes to daily surrender to God, Rudolf Otto, in *The Idea of the Holy,* captured a key concept that corresponds with "effortless effort" in his phrase *"mysterium tremendum."* The quiet, penetrating encounter with God in the depths of our being is possible only when we let him go. When we quit boxing him in, or calling him this or that, or trying to make him do things for us—*then* we are filled with his presence. It is by beholding his being, and asking nothing other than to be still in his presence, that we surrender to God.

We leave the encounter *moved* in our core, because we have

asked nothing and received everything. This is the mystery of the holiness and love of God. We can make one gentle step—practically effortless—and in so surrendering to God we are bountifully blessed. The quiet, daily surrender of one's innermost being to God brings peace and a progressive work of wholeness to one's life.

For the actualizing Christian, life is a balance and synthesis between inner contemplation and outer social action, between *being* and *doing.* The times of quiet, relaxed surrender and openness in the presence of God harmonize with times of interaction with family, friends, and the world at large. Busyness, planning, and doing also give way rhythmically to gentle meditation and prayer. This process assures that one's day-to-day involvements are inspired and brought to fruition by the gentle flow of God's Spirit in one's life.

Belief Versus Faith

Belief is the insistence in the here and now that *this* or *that* is what one values and subscribes to in terms of one's present limited experience. But it must be amplified by faith. Faith does not simply defend the truth as one now sees it, but faith is, in the words of Alan Watts, "an unreserved opening of the mind to the truth, whatever it may turn out to be." Faith involves a plunge into the unknown. Belief clings, but faith lets go.

This process of letting go of the old and taking hold of the new is a natural part of Christian growth. Just as the trapeze artist must have faith in order to synchronize his transition from one bar to the next, so the actualizing Christian must remain willing to depart from old ways in order to arrive at new ones. As the scripture says, "without faith it is impossible to please [God]" (Hebrews 11:6 RSV). But God is himself faithful. As Paul Tournier has said:

> There is no strength greater than that of God to help us to let go of the past, and to escape from its bonds. But that past was in fact the strong support that God gave to help us to leap forward towards him. (*A Place for You,* p. 201)

Time and again we must plunge beyond our manipulative and character patterns into the stream of energy from the core. This reduces the significance of the defensive structures and opens up the flow of energies from the wellspring of God within our core. The core unifies the polarities and heals the inner wounds of fear, releasing a flow of power that replaces fear of life with *faith in life.* Thus, faith becomes an important factor in growth.

Many "religious" people confuse faith with clinging to certain ideas. Growth as an actualizing Christian, it seems to us, requires death as well as rebirth—death to old ideas and beliefs. The new wine of the Christian's Spirit-led life must continuously be put into the fresh wineskins of new attitudes, perceptions, and values. We need the courage to communicate to others with whom we differ. We also need the courage to shed old preconceptions. Faith requires an opening of ourselves to new ideas and experiences, and a willingness to let outworn and partial ideas of truth die. This is growth in the finest sense of the word. This is what Tillich means by "the courage to doubt"—the courage to *entertain* differences in the hope that one may learn new and more satisfying ways of viewing truth. Catholic philosopher Gabriel Marcel writes in *Creative Fidelity*: "Authentic Christian thought is an open thought *par excellence.* . . . A real orthodoxy creates those conditions rooted in the supernatural which unfold the most spacious and unbounded horizons for human knowledge and action."

To conclude, the actualizing Christian must have the courage to embrace insecurity and doubt. This person is the opposite of the fanatic, who attacks with disproportionate violence those who disagree. The actualizing Christian has the "courage to be" in spite of doubts, which are valued because they can help growth. We should try not to be like the neurotic, who builds a narrow castle of certitude defended with the utmost tenacity. Rather we should continue to express and to ask, so that we can receive answers in our areas of doubt—knowing that some answers do not come easily. We have *faith* that by "asking, seeking, and knocking," we will eventually have the answers revealed in our life situation.

Living in the Here and Now

The actualizing Christian learns how to live in the here and now, while trusting the past and future to God. What has happened in the past, one accepts, not hanging on to the good or bad experiences. One takes what one has learned from all experiences, uses that wisdom from then on, and leaves the experiences themselves in the past. One is free, then, of the burden of guilt, resentment, embarrassment, despair, or bitterness that being stuck in past memories would cause.

In regard to the future, one takes the responsibility to make tentative plans, yet trusts the final outcome of each day and each year to God. One takes to heart the saying of Christ to "seek ye first the kingdom of God, and his righteousness; and all these things shall be added unto you" (Matthew 6:33). One has faith in the future without having to make rigid and unrealistic goals. One gives up demanding a guarantee from God or anyone else just exactly how things will work out in one's life. Instead, one chooses to do what one can and trusts God for the rest. This style of life bears the fruit of peace, joy, and contentment. Even though there are sudden reversals or traumas or things one did not count on, one looks to God to reveal in time a deeper meaning for why things turn out the way they do. So, again, one discovers a sense of peace in even the most turbulent times. This is not to say that the Christian does not experience anxiety, confusion, or frustration. Rather, it is simply to say that underneath these feelings will remain a depth of calm and peace, just as the ocean remains calm underneath the turbulent waves of a hurricane. The source of calmness is the person's deep-rootedness in the Spirit of God.

Author's personal comment—Ev:
This past year several things happened to me so suddenly that I did not know which way to turn. I felt jarred. I know that

my blood pressure even went up as I tried to understand how to handle certain relationships and circumstances.

Dan and I spent time in prayer, and I deeply yielded my life to God, so that I could learn what he was expecting of me and which direction I should go. Out of this surrender came a real peace. I had an inner assurance that things would work out in the best way.

Even though I feel worried occasionally, I have already begun to realize that God is answering my prayers, and that his hand is in all that is happening to me. So I am trusting God in each moment and not trying to predict or manipulate the future. I am experiencing faith to let things go so that God can decide what the future holds.

The actualizing Christian seeks a balance in which he or she lives fully and responsively in the present, yet ties the past and the future to the present in a meaningful continuity. This life-style is in accord with the biblical invitations to trust God in all things and to praise him however things might be turning out. The testimony of Scripture is that even the most seemingly tragic events are changed into the most stunning victories for those who put their trust in God.

Actualizing Love

On the foundation of emotional and spiritual freedom, the actualizing Christian needs to build bridges to others. Love of self and love of others are meant to run parallel. As Fritz Perls has said:

The harmonious functioning of the individual and society depends upon: "Thou shalt love thy neighbor as thyself." Not less, but also not more. Only when he learns to strike the balance between egoism and altruism—between identification with his own and other people's requirements—will he find peace of mind. (*Ego, Hunger, and Aggression*, p. 224)

Giving and taking are both vital parts of loving in an actualizing manner. We do not grow by either giving all the

124

time or receiving all the time. Both are needed for balanced relationships with others. This means both being able to stand on our own feet *and* reaching out to others. It means being able to handle a certain degree of aloneness *and* desiring the company of others. It means having a sense of personal power *and* choosing to bare our deepest heart in love to others.

As actualizing Christians, we should be humble enough to ask for and receive help when it is needed. At the same time, we should be able to handle many things for ourselves. We should learn to take responsibility for our own fulfillment, yet be able to look beyond ourselves and, whenever possible, give freely to meet the needs of others.

We go through life becoming both more capable and more aware of our limitations and needs. This is the pathway of genuine *inter*dependence, a crucial dynamic of actualizing love.

Another dimension of maintaining balance in relationships is giving up our need to be "right" all the time. We must become more willing to honestly *express* ourselves, *listen* to others, and *learn* from one another, rather than always judging who's "right" and who's "wrong." If we can learn to "agree to disagree" with one another, then love will flow freely even when there are great differences among people. One measure of the strength of love is the extent to which it, like glue, brings the most diverse elements together in a common bond.

The actualizing Christian learns to relate respectfully to other people without judging them harshly or rejecting them. Love enables us to seek to understand others, and every person is worth understanding.

The actualizing Christian recognizes the privilege of Jews, Buddhists, atheists, agnostics, and even other Christians to be different. Openness to others who are different replaces defensiveness; yet in one's own core, the Christian can still radiate the presence of Christ in the world.

But the opposite of love is a *fear of loving.* As we stressed earlier in this book, fear can constrict one into nonloving. To be committed to the well-being of ourselves and others means cutting through fear to make a commitment, without guarantee that our love will be returned. This requires the courage to risk possibly facing some pain and disappointment, because there will be many who will not return the love or will even return disdain instead. We must have the courage to accept that we will occasionally be hurt in our attempts to truly love others. Yet, we can realize that the joy and fulfillment of love in our life makes it worth coping with the hurt and vulnerability that sometimes happen.

13. Coming Home to the Core

> *You order all things graciously. You are the mystery unfolding cosmos and humanity. You are my homeland, my most original ground. Your Presence welds all things together. You are the caring love that carries me like mother earth does forest, flower, and tree. Your Presence alone is lasting home.*
> —*Adrian van Kaam*

To change fear into perfect loving requires a clear definition of *grace*. Perhaps the most profound type of core experience comes in what it means to be "struck by grace." By grace we mean the *gift* of God that we are loved and accepted without effort on our part. It is often referred to as *unmerited* love from God. Paul Tillich describes this experience:

Do we know what it means to be struck by grace? It happens; or it does not happen. Grace strikes us when we are in great pain and restlessness. It strikes us when we walk through the dark valley of a meaningless and empty life. It strikes us when we feel our separation is deeper than usual. . . . It strikes us when our disgust for our own being, our indifference, our weakness, our hostility, and our lack of direction and composure have become intolerable to us. It strikes us when, year after year, the longed-for perfection of life does not appear. . . . At that moment . . . it is as though a voice were saying: *"You are accepted,"* accepted by that which is greater than you. . . . After such an experience we may not be better than before, and we may not believe more than before. But everything is transformed. (*The Shaking of the Foundations,* pp. 161-62)

It is through grace, the *in-flowing* of God's love, that we become able to love our neighbor from the great reservoir of God-given love within.

When we are blessed with grace, we find ourselves loved and affirmed in such a way that we love God and others more than ever. The Christian may receive this grace through prayer, inspiration from the Scriptures, meditation, church services, or daily Spirit-led interaction with others. But the essential ingredient, which then becomes an irreversible aspect of our own core, is that such love is by nature unmerited—we are loved by the grace of God, not because of our achievements or what we do. We are simply loved. And such love radiates outward in the same way. Others need not merit our love—we simply love them, too. One is most grace-full when one experiences others in their essential core, loving them as purely as God does.

Once we have accepted this grace, then ancillary virtues follow. Such qualities as caring, respect, and responsibility flow from this fountainhead of life within. We can always receive a boundless affirmation of love from deep within. It is grace, which is given us by God and finds a regal home in our core, the kingdom of God within. God becomes to us a deep and ever-present Companion.

The center of healthy psychological and spiritual growth is the core, or innermost being, of the person. The core is not the raw, chaotic power of the unconscious that Freud portrayed. Rather, it is an innate guidance system energized by the power of God's love. It is out of our core that dignity, courage, and love emerge that we might live life to the fullest. The subtle nuances of guidance that flow from the core enable a person to become truly human, and to fulfill his or her unique mission in life.

We might understand the core as the place of divine support within the personality. Tournier wrote in *A Place for You,* "God is always there, always available, and for everyone, both small and great, unbelievers as well as believers, rebels as well as those who obey Him."

Our spirituality is our movement from and into the core. The core is the involuntary energy center *into* which flows the love of God and *from* which flows love for oneself and others. As Paul says, "God's love has been poured into our hearts through the Holy Spirit" (Romans 5:5 RSV). Thus, love is expressed through the core, and love becomes central to our understanding of the core.

We see the verse "Thou shalt love the Lord thy God with all thy heart, and with all thy soul, and with all thy strength, and with all thy mind; and thy neighbor as thyself" (Luke 10:27) as the key to being an actualizing Christian. If we love God first, then God can work through us most profoundly at our cores to assist us in loving our neighbors as ourselves. The idea expressed in this verse may be diagrammed as follows:

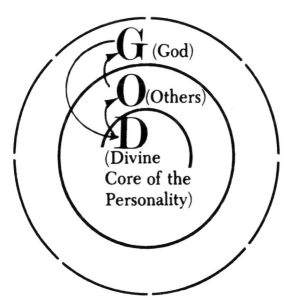

Figure 8: THE FLOW OF ACTUALIZING LOVE

As implied in Figure 8, *God,* by his unmerited grace, expresses himself to the Christian through the person's core. One may then express what God is manifesting within oneself outward to others. We begin to understand the importance of the core, and why we call it a "divine core," when we see it as our purest connection with God.

It is a premise of this book that the primary *interpersonal* method through which God expresses himself is through the presence of the Holy Spirit. Van Kaam writes:

> All the love our Father and Jesus communicate to humanity is given through the Spirit. The Spirit is the Holy One in his infinite generosity, in his boundless self communication. He is divine sharing. Knowing him is that quiet awareness of his touch, tender as the morning dew on flowers opening up for the dawn. (*Looking for Jesus,* p. 117)

As shown in Figure 8, we believe that the Holy Spirit expresses the presence of God within the human personality. God's loving will becomes incarnate in the human situation when his love flows freely *through* a person *into* others and *back to* God through feelings of gratitude and praise. Thus the cycle is completed and God is able to permeate, transform, and elevate each life that is open to him.

Elizabeth O'Connor has said that prayerful surrender to God from the core of one's being brings about a "fundamental change" in the quality of a person's life, so that life comes to be lived on an entirely different level of existence. She writes:

> Mysterious as this may sound, it actually has to do with changes in very ordinary aspects of living, such as increased awareness of what we see and hear, a heightened degree of receptivity, a growing capacity to respond—to be engaged in the moment as one who is fully present. (*Search for Silence,* p. 114)

Coming home to one's core involves surrendering to the quiet inner wisdom of the mysterious, bedrock presence of the Holy Spirit within one's life and personality. King Solomon was aware of this when he wrote: "For wisdom will enter the very center of your being, filling your life with joy" (Proverbs 2:10 TLB).

Living from this core, the actualizing Christian exemplifies a new dimension of openness to life in the following ways. He or she becomes:

1. *An adventurer in truth.* One sees life as an adventure in becoming oneself as fully as Christ was himself in his life.
2. *An expresser of one's own Christlikeness.* Because one believes in the kingdom of God within, one's goal is to express grace-fully and in an original way the particular talents, gifts, or ministries that one has been given by God.
3. *An enlightened traveler on the road of life.* One's core represents a light within. It is a light that each person must discover. The actualizing Christian can make his or her light shine so as to guide others to discover their own inner light. As Jesus said, "You are the light of the world. . . . Let your light so shine before men, that they may see your good works, and give glory to your Father who is in heaven" (Matthew 5:14, 16 RSV).

The kind of full and intimate surrender to God that we have been talking about may seem difficult for some readers to understand. Yet the message of the New Testament is that union with Christ by the power of the Holy Spirit is the calling of every Christian and the meaning of true spirituality. It then becomes highly feasible to speak of the inner core of the personality as being filled with the Holy Spirit. And the overflow of that "infilling" is a lifetime of graced relationships with others.

One of the New Testament Greek words used for the Holy Spirit is *Paracletos.* This translates as "one called alongside to help" or "comforter" or "companion." These meanings clearly indicate a most personal and intimate role of the Holy Spirit in supporting, nurturing, and guiding a person through life.

In addition, as we wrote in chapter 6, Jesus promised the gift of the Holy Spirit to those who accepted and followed him (John 14:18). He portrayed the Holy Spirit as the believer's personal Companion who would be adequate for all the needs of daily life. We encourage the reader who is unfamiliar with these references to read or reread the four Gospels and the Book of Acts, found at the beginning of the New Testament.

As we move further in the process of integrating the Bible with psychology, we can say that the Holy Spirit is intended by God to be the center of our existence—the inspiration of our feelings, thoughts, choices, and values. "Out of this oneness," writes van Kaam, "flow forth the works of God. He asks us to lend him our eyes to see, our mouth to speak, our ears to hear, our mind to think, our heart to love, our feet to walk, our hands to act" (*Looking for Jesus,* p. 92).

We would say that genuine spirituality, for the Christian or anyone else, is responding to the Spirit of God and *doing* God's will. This is the surrender that we have been talking about throughout the book. This is the surrender of one's whole being to the will of God. We do not believe that it is a once-and-for-all event as much as it is a continuous day-by-day process.

The Well Within

How is it possible that the fear behind our manipulations, character disorders, and even psychoses described in this book can be healed by the perfect love of God? We believe that the key to understanding this is the awareness that the actualizing Christian, in being filled and led by the Holy Spirit, lives in an atmosphere of *inspiration* rather than condemnation.

According to Webster's, *to perfect* means "to bring to final form." *Our fears are healed when we realize that we are being enabled by God's Spirit within to perfect our love of ourselves, others, and God.* We no longer fear punishment because we know that we are partners with God in developing our capacity to be all we are meant to be—and to love our neighbors as ourselves.

The artesian well provides an excellent analogy for understanding the human personality. An artesian well is a well

132

drilled deep enough to reach water that has converged underground from a source originally higher than the well itself. Therefore, the water that flows into the well has a natural pressure upward that forces it through the well. (See Figure 9.)

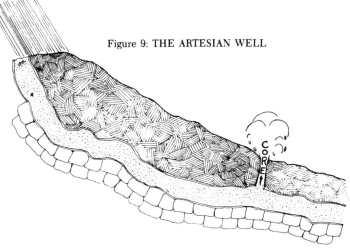

Figure 9: THE ARTESIAN WELL

All that is required to keep the well filled to overflowing is the continued release of its water. This keeps the core of the well cleansed and open, allowing fresh water to always flow through. Here we see the great importance of developing a *giving attitude* in life.

So it is with us in our reliance on the flow of God's Spirit, a Source greater than ourselves, to flow through the core of our lives. If we receive freely from the abundance of God's inner provision, we will have much to give. In giving, our own wells are continually filled to overflowing. But not everyone receives the richness of God's love in the inner self. Some have not drilled deep enough; they have not fully surrendered to God as their Source. Others have begun to tap the unlimited supply within, but find that it quickly clogs up when fear constricts their giving attitude toward others.

But when we begin to understand how profoundly we are loved by God, we can begin to surrender in our innermost being to the gentle flow of the Spirit in our lives. Before long, we will experience firsthand the thrill of "stirrings deep within" as our inner core is filled to overflowing with the Holy Spirit.

This flow within gives us a sense of perfect peace, even though we know that we are not yet perfect. As the scripture says, "Thou wilt keep him in perfect peace, whose mind is stayed on thee, because he trusteth in thee" (Isaiah 26:3). As Christians, we can remain humble, and joyous, recognizing that our beings are vessels through which flows the Holy Spirit. It is the power of God, not our own power, that flows through us into our life and relationships.

Drinking deeply from the well within, and knowing that God is working each day to move us toward wholeness, truly creates a sense of "wellness." As the song says, "When peace like a river attendeth my soul . . . I know it is *well* with my soul."

It is our wish that this book be a testimony to others that they, too, may experience this peace. Jesus said, "He who believes in Me, . . . 'From his innermost being shall flow rivers of living water'" (John 7:38 NASB).

Bibliography

Assagioli, Roberto. *Psychosynthesis.* New York: Viking, 1965.

Bonhoeffer, Dietrich. *Ethics.* Trans. Eberhard Bethge. New York: Macmillan, 1965.

Frankl, Viktor. *Man's Search for Meaning.* New York: Simon & Schuster, 1959.

Graham, Billy. *How to Be Born Again.* Waco, Tex.: Word Books, 1977.

Horney, Karen. *Our Inner Conflicts.* New York: W. W. Norton, 1945.

Ladd, George. *A Theology of the New Testament.* Grand Rapids: Eerdmans, 1974.

Lazarus, Arnold. *Behavior Therapy and Beyond.* New York: McGraw-Hill, 1971.

Lindbergh, A. M. *Hour of Gold, Hour of Lead.* New York: Harcourt Brace Jovanovich, 1973.

Lowen, Alexander. *Bioenergetics.* New York: Coward, McCann & Geoghegan, 1975.

Marcel, Gabriel. *Creative Fidelity.* New York: Farrar, Straus, 1964.

Maslow, Abraham. *Motivation and Personality.* 2nd. ed. New York: Harper, 1970.

————. *Toward a Psychology of Being.* 2nd ed. New York: Van Nostrand, 1968.

May, Rollo. *Man's Search for Himself.* New York: Dell Publishing Co., 1973.

————. *The Art of Counseling.* Nashville: Abingdon Apex Book, 1967.

Menninger, Karl A. *Love Against Hate.* New York: Harcourt, Brace paperback, 1959.

Merton, Thomas. *No Man Is an Island.* New York: Harcourt, Brace, 1955.

O'Connor, Elizabeth. *Search for Silence.* Waco, Tex.: Word Books, 1972.

Osborne, Cecil. *The Art of Learning to Love Yourself.* Grand Rapids: Zondervan, 1976.

Otto, Rudoph. *The Idea of the Holy.* Trans. John Harvey. 2nd ed. New York: Oxford University Press paperback, 1958.

Perls, F. S. *Ego, Hunger, and Aggression: The Beginning of Gestalt Therapy.* New York: Random House paperback, 1969.

Rogers, Carl. *Counseling and Psychotherapy.* Boston: Houghton Mifflin, 1942.

————. *On Becoming a Person.* Boston: Houghton Mifflin, 1961.

Runyon, Theodore, ed. *What the Spirit Is Saying to the Churches.* New York: Hawthorn Books, 1975.

Schaeffer, Francis. *True Spirituality.* Wheaton, Ill.: Tyndale House, 1971.

Shostrom, Everett. *Actualizing Therapy: Foundations for a Scientific Ethic.* San Diego: EDITS, 1976.

————. *Man the Manipulator.* Nashville: Abingdon, 1967.

Stuart, Grace. *Narcissus: A Psychological Study of Self-Love.* New York: Macmillan, 1955.

Tillich, Paul. *The New Being.* New York: Scribner's, 1955.

————. *The Shaking of the Foundations.* New York: Scribner's, 1948.

Tournier, Paul. *A Place for You.* Trans. Edwin Hudson. New York: Harper, 1968.

Van Kaam, Adrian. *Spirituality and the Gentle Life.* Denville, N. J.: Dimension Books, 1974.

————. *Looking for Jesus.* Denville, N. J.: Dimension Books, 1978.

————. *The Woman at the Well.* Denville, N. J.: Dimension Books, 1976.

Vetter, Bernadette. *My Journey, My Prayer.* New York: Wm. H. Sadlier, 1977.

Index

Subject Index